MW00885129

BE AGILE®

Agile Requirements and User Stories

Part of the Agile Education Series™

CAPE PROJECT
MANAGEMENT, INC.

CAPE PROJECT
MANAGEMENT, INC.

2

Introductions and Expectations

Copyrighted material. 2018

CAPE PROJECT
MANAGEMENT, INC.

Agile Requirements Affinity Mapping

Copyrighted material. 2018

CAPE PROJECT
MANAGEMENT, INC.

About Us

- ▸ The course curriculum developed by Dan Tousignant, PMI-ACP, CSP, PSPO of Cape Project Management, Inc.
- ▸ We provide public, onsite and online training:
  - ◦ AgileProjectManagementTraining.com
- ▸ Follow us on Twitter @ScrumDan

Copyrighted material. 2018  CAPE PROJECT MANAGEMENT, INC.

The Agile Education Series™

1. Scrum Master Certification Training
2. Product Owner and User Story Training
3. All About Agile™: PMI-ACP® Agile Exam Preparation
4. Kanban for Software Development Teams
5. Achieving Agility – How to implement Agile in your organization
6. Agile for Team Members
7. Agile for Executives

- ▸ All of these curriculums are available on Amazon at:
  - ◦ http://bit.ly/DansAgileBooks

Copyrighted material. 2018  CAPE PROJECT MANAGEMENT, INC.

Continuing Education

- This course provides education credits for the following certifications:
  - Continuing Certification for PMPs & PMI-ACPs: 7 PDUs Category B: Continuing Education
  - PMI-ACP Application: 7 Agile Education Contact Hours
  - Scrum Alliance SEUs for CSP Application and Maintenance: 7 SEUS Category C: Outside Events
  - Certified Business Analysis Professional (CBAP): 7 Hours of Professional Development

  CAPE PROJECT MANAGEMENT, INC.

Course Objectives

- Gain a thorough understanding of the use of the Agile Product Lifecycle, Agile Requirements and User Stories
- Have fun!

  CAPE PROJECT MANAGEMENT, INC.

Agenda

Modules
1. The Agile Product Lifecycle
2. Agile Requirements
3. *Agile Prioritizing*
4. *Agile Sizing and Estimating*

Announcements

- ▸ Materials
  - ◦ Slides
  - ◦ Exercises
  - ◦ Group Activities
- ▸ Breaks

CAPE PROJECT
MANAGEMENT, INC.

11

(Agile Onion)

The Agile Product Lifecycle

Module 1

CAPE PROJECT
MANAGEMENT, INC.

12

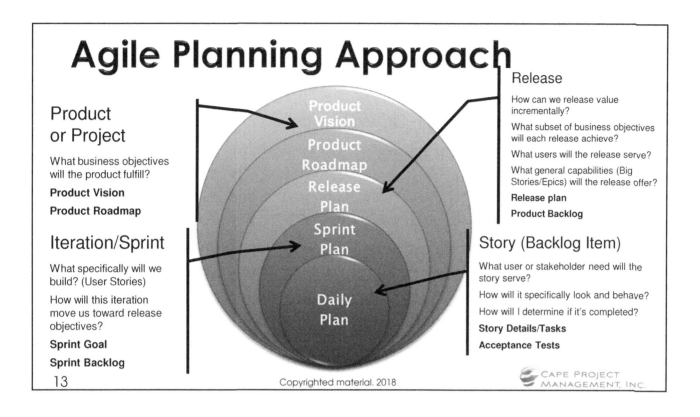

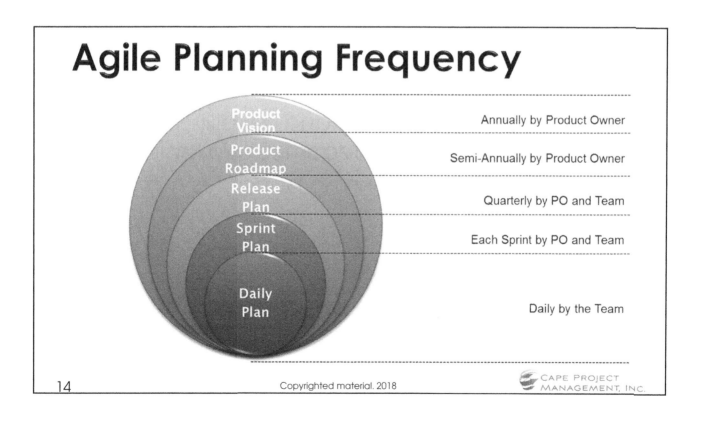

Agile Plans

▸ Typically are top-down
▸ Are easy to change
▸ Limit dependencies
▸ Follow a rolling-wave approach
  ◦ Rolling Wave Planning is a technique that enables you to plan for a project as it unfolds. This technique requires you to plan iteratively. You plan until you have more visibility and then re-plan.

15 Copyrighted material. 2018  CAPE PROJECT MANAGEMENT, INC.

Progressive Elaboration

▸ Continuously improving and detailing a plan as more information becomes available
▸ Each iteration of planning becomes more accurate
▸ Use information from each release to support plan for next release

16 Copyrighted material. 2018  CAPE PROJECT MANAGEMENT, INC.

Creating a Product Vision

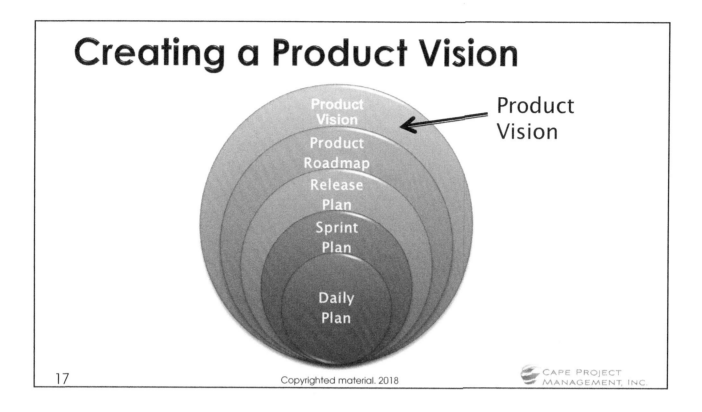

Product Vision

Copyrighted material. 2018  CAPE PROJECT MANAGEMENT, INC.

Developing a Vision

- ‣ The product vision is key to the success of the project.
- ‣ The product vision should align with the company vision
- ‣ The vision should be revisited frequently
- ‣ All releases of the product should related back to the vision

Copyrighted material. 2018 CAPE PROJECT MANAGEMENT, INC.

Effective Vision Statements

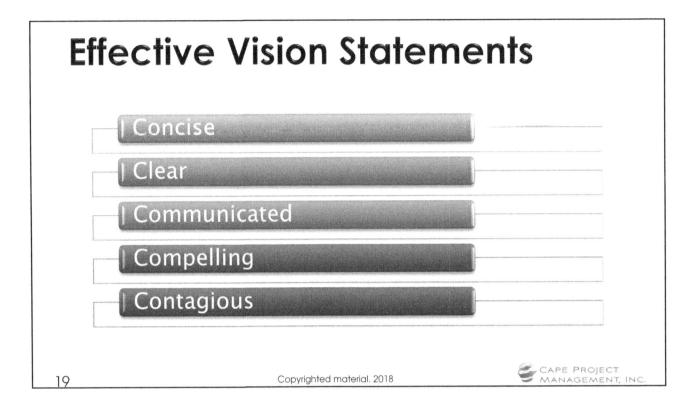

CAPE PROJECT
MANAGEMENT, INC.

Effective Vision Statements

- **Concise**: An effective vision statement must be short and simple so it can be understood and articulated by everyone in the organization.
- **Clear**: Lack of clarity may be the single greatest failure of a healthy vision.
- **Communicated**: A vision statement can be concise and clear, but unless it is communicated well, it has little power.
- **Compelling**: You should be able to see clearly in the vision statement something that will naturally move people toward greater commitment and decisive actions.
- **Contagious**: The vision statement should be something that makes the organization proud.

CAPE PROJECT
MANAGEMENT, INC.

Effective Vision Statements

"Our vision is to be earth's most customer centric company; to build a place where people can come to find and discover anything they might want to buy online."

"Making the best possible ice cream, in the nicest possible way"

"Give customers the freshest, highest quality foods you can buy and provide them with friendly service in a sparkling clean environment."

21

CAPE PROJECT
MANAGEMENT, INC.

Company Vision vs. Product Vision

Company Vision
▸ Our goal is to make learning more desirable, accessible, and meaningful for learners. By doing this, we have a shared sense of purpose with teachers, administrators, and leaders at all levels that are working to improve outcomes for learners.

Product Vision
▸ The Learning Management System (LMS) will enhance the educational experience by giving students and educators more ways to stay engaged online - both in and outside of the classroom. It will give students and faculty access to their courses, content, and grading and will allow them to participate in an online learning community on their desktop and variety of mobile devices.

22

CAPE PROJECT
MANAGEMENT, INC.

Create a Vision Board

Vision: What is your overarching goal for creating the product?			
Product	Needs	Target Group	Value
What is the product? What makes it desirable? Is it feasible to develop?	What problem does the product solve? What benefit does it provide?	Who are the target users and customers?	How is the product going to benefit the company? What are the business goals?

Source: http://www.romanpichler.com/blog/the-product-vision-board/

 CAPE PROJECT
MANAGEMENT, INC.

23

Vision Board Example

Vision: The Learning Management System (LMS) will enhance the educational experience by giving students and educators more ways to stay engaged online – both in and outside of the classroom. It will give students and faculty access to their courses, content, and grading and will allow them to participate in an online learning community on their desktop and variety of mobile devices.			
Product	Needs	Target Group	Value
Online access to courses, grading, and student profiles. Eliminates paper and provides platform for collaboration. Development team and expertise exists.	Eliminates the need for paper catalogs, add/drop forms and high involvement of faculty. Reduces overhead, 24/7 access and ability to change content.	Students Faculty Administrators Parents	Customer base is every university, school, and training organization in the world. Generate revenue with each release of functionality.

24

CAPE PROJECT
MANAGEMENT, INC.

Group Exercise: Create a Vision Board

1. Select a Case Study
    a. Provide a site to store all cross departmental documents, maintain public personnel profiles, support internal blogs, and provided external and public viewing of program status and progress against departmental objectives.
    b. Create a social networking site that combines the concept of Meetups, dating, and event planning for those people interested in outdoor activities.
    c. Design and build new cafeteria for your building that that meets the needs of your organization and is also a profit center to draw external customers.
2. Create a Vision Board with your team
3. Be prepared to share with the class

Product Name:

Vision Statement:

Product	Needs	Target Group	Value

Vision: What is your overarching goal for creating the product?

Product	Needs	Target Group	Value
What is the product? What makes it desirable? Is it feasible to develop?	What problem does the product solve? What benefit does it provide?	Who are the target users and customers?	How is the product going to benefit the company? What are the business goals?

Vision: The Learning Management System (LMS) will enhance the educational experience by giving students and educators more ways to stay engaged online – both in and outside of the classroom. It will give students and faculty access to their courses, content, and grading and will allow them to participate in an online learning community on their desktop and variety of mobile devices.

Product	Needs	Target Group	Value
Online access to courses, grading, and student profiles. Eliminates paper and provides platform for collaboration. Development team and expertise exists.	Eliminates the need for paper catalogs, add/drop forms and high involvement of faculty. Reduces overhead, 24/7 access and ability to change content.	Students Faculty Administrators Parents	Customer base is every university, school, and training organization in the world. Generate revenue with each release of functionality.

GROUP EXERCISE

Exercise 1
Create a Product Vision Board

Copyrighted material. 2018 CAPE PROJECT MANAGEMENT, INC.

Roadmap Planning

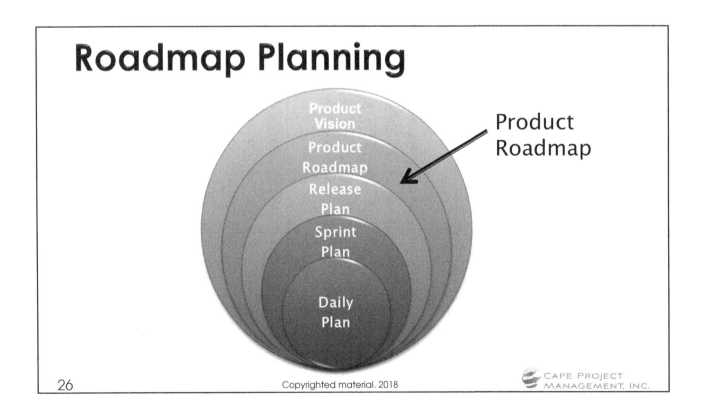

Product Roadmap

Copyrighted material. 2018 CAPE PROJECT MANAGEMENT, INC.

Product Roadmap

- A roadmap is a planned future, laid out in broad strokes
  - Planned or proposed product releases, listing high level functionality or release themes, laid out in rough timeframes
  - For a period usually extending for 2 or 3 significant feature releases into the future
- Shows progress towards strategy
- Lots of "wiggle room"
- Example:
  - Implement course listing functionality
  - Implement grading functionality
  - Implement discussion groups
  - Implement student profiles

27   Copyrighted material. 2018    CAPE PROJECT MANAGEMENT, INC.

Product Roadmap Example

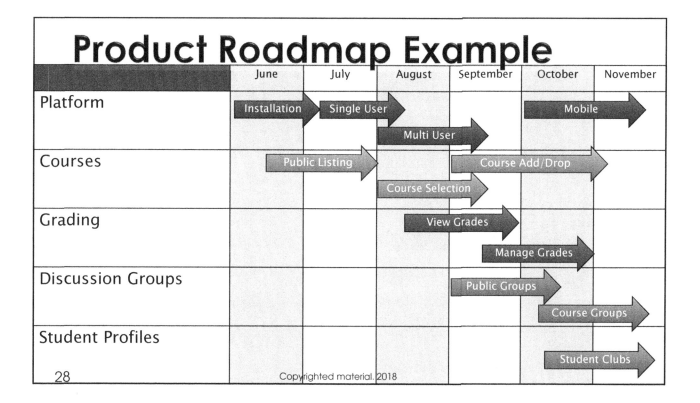

	June	July	August	September	October	November
Platform	Installation	Single User	Multi User		Mobile	
Courses		Public Listing	Course Selection	Course Add/Drop		
Grading			View Grades	Manage Grades		
Discussion Groups				Public Groups	Course Groups	
Student Profiles					Student Clubs	

28   Copyrighted material. 2018

Product Roadmap

Theme/Timescale

GROUP EXERCISE

Exercise 2
Product Roadmap

Release Planning

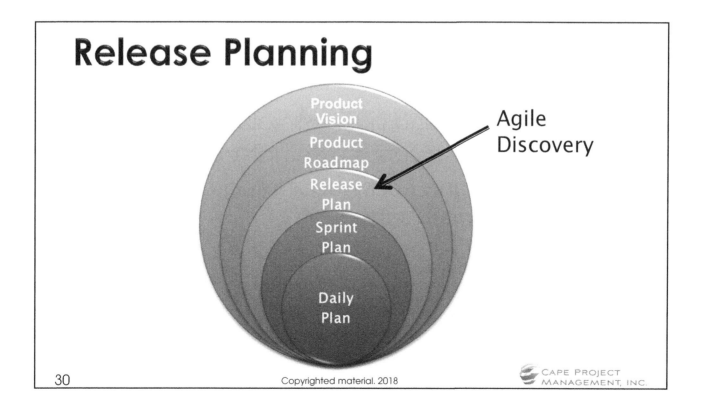

Agile Discovery

- **Desired Business Outcomes:** Document outcomes that are quantifiable and measurable.
- **High Level Architecture**: Outline a plan for the technical and business architecture/design of the solution.
- **High Level Delivery Plan**: Segment the solution into the smallest minimum viable products (MVPs) that realize the desired outcomes and sets out the order in which they are to be delivered.
- **Product Backlog**: Create an evolving prioritized list of all items of work which may be relevant to the solution.
- **Governance Approach**: Describe essential governance and organization aspects of the project and how the project will be managed.
- **High-Level Budget**: Create a project budget and release budget to support resource planning and scheduling.

CAPE PROJECT
MANAGEMENT, INC.

Release Options

- Organized around business value
- Internal release versus external release
- Daily builds and continuous integration versus planned release schedule

CAPE PROJECT
MANAGEMENT, INC.

Minimum Viable Product (MVP)

▸ The product with the highest return on investment versus risk.

▸ Just those core features that allow the product to be deployed, and no more.

▸ It allows you to test an idea by exposing an early version of your product to the target users and customers, to collect the relevant data, and to learn from it.

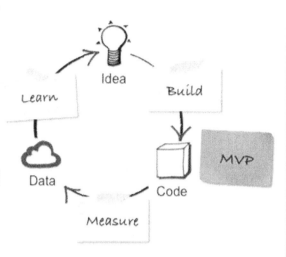

Source: http://www.romanpichler.com/blog/minimum-viable-product-and-minimal-marketable-product/

33   Copyrighted material. 2018   CAPE PROJECT MANAGEMENT, INC.

A Product Release Plan

▸ Goes into next level of detail
▸ Sets a common understanding
▸ A projection, not a commitment
▸ Example
   ◦ Release 1:
      · LMS Installed with pilot group logins validated
      · Pilot with 3 faculty and 60 students
      · Course listings available
   ◦ Release 2
      · Incorporate pilot feedback
      · Enable College of Engineering faculty and students
      · Implement course selection on-line
   ◦ Release 3
      · …

34   Copyrighted material. 2018   CAPE PROJECT MANAGEMENT, INC.

Release Plans

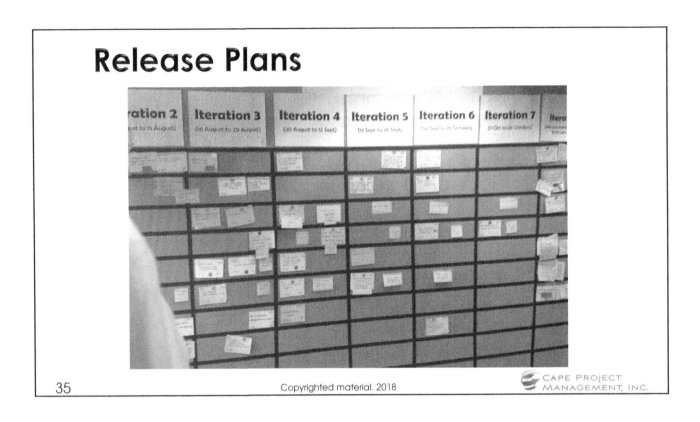

CAPE PROJECT
MANAGEMENT, INC.

Release Plans

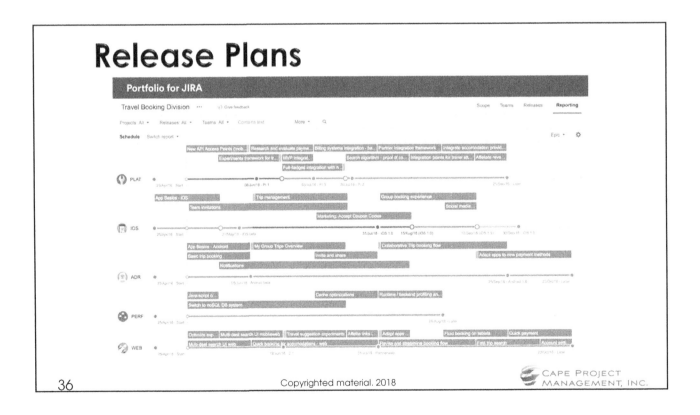

CAPE PROJECT
MANAGEMENT, INC.

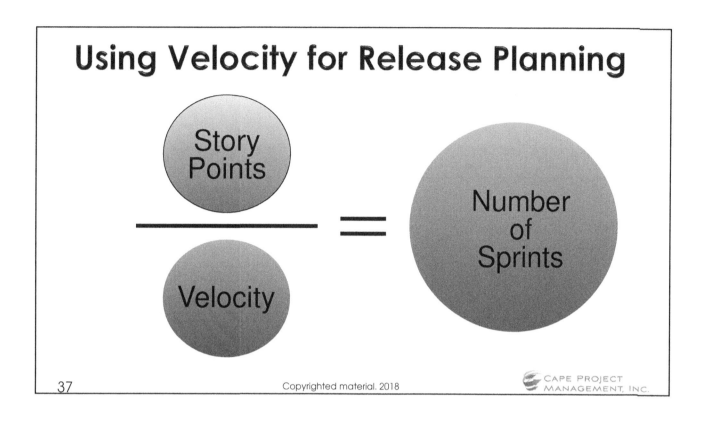

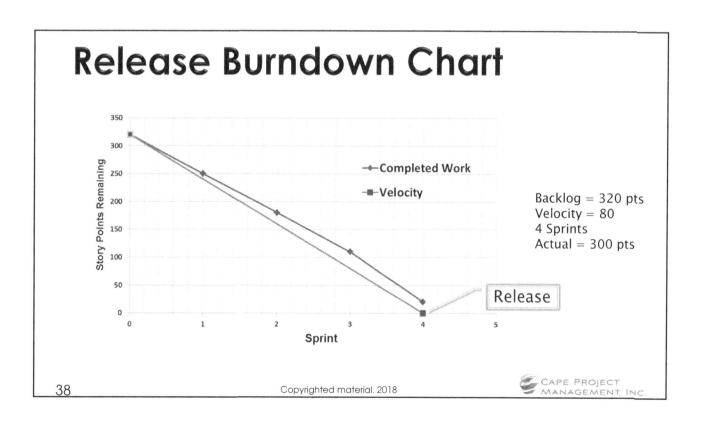

Group Exercise: Release Plan

Directions:
1. Return to your groups that developed vision and roadmap for the Case Study
2. Review your Roadmap
3. Identify your Minimum Viable Product (MVP) for next 3-5 releases
4. List your release plan below

Release Plan:

GROUP EXERCISE

Exercise 3
Create Release Plan
Define your MVP for 3 Releases

Copyrighted material. 2018

CAPE PROJECT MANAGEMENT, INC.

Priority:	Size:
As a:	
I want to:(what)	
So that: (why)	

Agile
Requirements
and User Stories
Module 2

Copyrighted material. 2018

CAPE PROJECT MANAGEMENT, INC.

Requirements Management

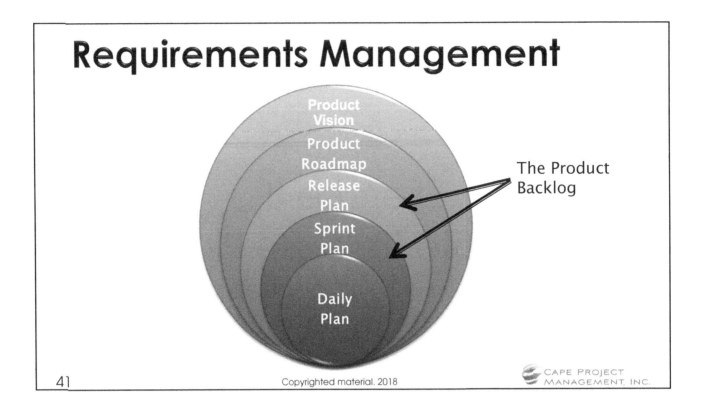

The Product Backlog

Copyrighted material. 2018  CAPE PROJECT MANAGEMENT, INC.

Product Owner's Role

- ▸ Single owner of the Product Backlog
- ▸ Maximizes the value (ROI) of the Product Backlog
- ▸ Determines how to order the Product Backlog but can delegate this function
- ▸ Ensures the Product Backlog is transparent to the entire organization
- ▸ Makes certain the backlog is "ready' for the Sprint Planning (otherwise Sprint is canceled)

Copyrighted material. 2018 CAPE PROJECT MANAGEMENT, INC.

Types of Backlogs

Type/View	Definition
Product	Set of prioritized requirements aligning with product vision
Release	The minimum requirements that would support a release. • Smallest possible release contains one Sprint • "Done–Done"
Sprint	A subset of requirements selected according to the velocity (capacity) of the team

Make the Product Backlog DEEP

▸ **Detailed Appropriately.** User stories on the product backlog that will be done soon need to be sufficiently well understood that they can be completed in the coming sprint. Stories to be developed later should be described with less detail.

▸ **Estimated.** The product backlog is more than a list of all work to be done; it is also a useful planning tool. Because items further down the backlog are not as well understood (yet), the estimates associated with them will be less precise than estimates given items at the top.

▸ **Emergent.** A product backlog is not static. It will change over time. As more is learned, user stories on the product backlog will be added, removed, or reprioritized.

▸ **Prioritized.** The product backlog should be sorted with the most valuable items at the top and the least valuable at the bottom. By always working in priority order, the team is able to maximize the value of the product or system being developed.

Roman Pichler, author of "*Agile Product Management with Scrum: Creating Products That Customers Love*"

Creating a Product Backlog

1. Create requirements or User Stories
2. Prioritize Requirements based upon Roadmap and Release Plan
3. Estimate Requirements
4. Update every Sprint – Backlog refinement
5. Consider a requirements hierarchy

45   Copyrighted material. 2018  CAPE PROJECT MANAGEMENT, INC.

Agile Requirements Hierarchy

46   Copyrighted material. 2018  CAPE PROJECT MANAGEMENT, INC.

Themes, Epics and User Stories

Themes
▸ Themes are groups of related stories. Often the stories all contribute to a common goal or are related in some obvious way, such as all focusing on a single function.

Epics
▸ Epics resemble themes in the sense that they are made up of multiple stories. As opposed to themes, however, these stories often comprise a complete workflow for a user.

User Stories
▸ A User story is a self-contained unit of work agreed upon by the developers and the stakeholders. Stories are the building blocks of your sprint.

CAPE PROJECT
MANAGEMENT, INC.

Themes, Epics and User Stories

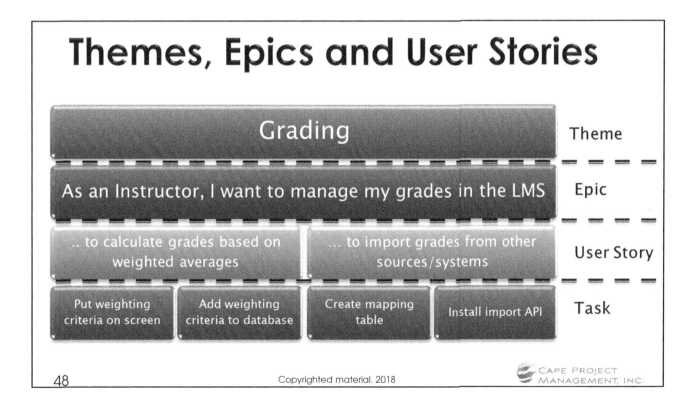

CAPE PROJECT
MANAGEMENT, INC.

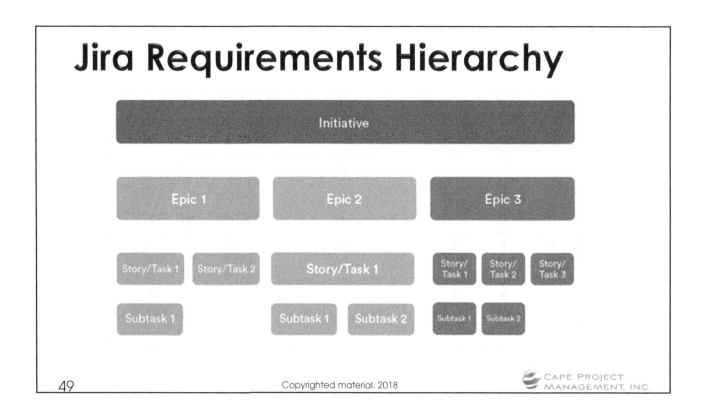

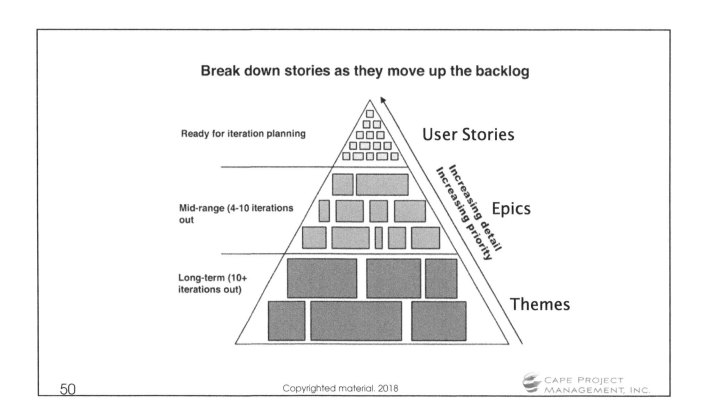

Requirements Considerations

- ▸ Written requirements
  - ◦ can be well thought through, reviewed and edited
  - ◦ provide a permanent record
  - ◦ are easily shared with groups of people
  - ◦ time consuming to produce
  - ◦ may be less relevant or superseded over time
  - ◦ can be easily misinterpreted
- ▸ Verbal requirements
  - ◦ instantaneous feedback and clarification
  - ◦ information-packed exchange
  - ◦ easier to clarify and gain common understanding
  - ◦ easily adapted to any new information known at the time
  - ◦ can spark ideas about problems and opportunities
  - ◦ can be vague if they are not validated

51   Copyrighted material. 2018   

Key Principles for Agile Requirements

- ▸ Active user involvement is imperative
- ▸ Agile teams must be empowered to make decisions
- ▸ Requirements emerge and evolve as software is developed
- ▸ Agile requirements are 'barely sufficient'
- ▸ Requirements are developed in small pieces
- ▸ Enough is enough – apply the 80/20 rule
- ▸ Cooperation, collaboration and communication between all team members is essential
- ▸ All requirements as captured in as product backlog items (PBIs)
- ▸ Agile requirements are often written as User Stories

52   Copyrighted material. 2018   

User Stories
seek to combine the strengths of written and verbal communication, where possible supported by a picture.

* Kent Beck coined the term user stories in Extreme Programming Explained 1st Edition, 1999

53

CAPE PROJECT MANAGEMENT, INC.

Agile Requirements - User Stories

- Agreement between customer and developer to have a conversation.
- A User Story is a very high-level definition of a requirement.
- Contains just enough information to produce a reasonable estimate of the effort to implement it.
- Product Owner writes User Stories on behalf of customer
  - Written in language of business to allow prioritization
  - Customer is primary product visionary

54

CAPE PROJECT MANAGEMENT, INC.

User Stories have 3 parts

Card *What is the goal of a user*	**As a (user role), I want to (goal) so I can (reason)** *Example:* *As a registered student, I want to view course details so I can create my schedule*
Conversation *How to achieve the goal using the system?*	**Discuss the card with a stakeholder. Just in time analysis (JIT) through conversations.** *Example:* *What information is needed to search for a course?* *What information is displayed?*
Confirmation *How to verify if the story is done and complete, and the goal is achieved*	**Record what you learn in an acceptance test.** *Example:* *Student can access course catalog 24 x 7 hours* *Student cannot choose more than three courses*

http://ronjeffries.com/xprog/articles/expcardconversationconfirmation/

Copyrighted material. 2018  CAPE PROJECT MANAGEMENT, INC.

User Story Cards - Front

Priority:		Size:

As a:
I want to:(what)

So that: (why)

Copyrighted material. 2018 CAPE PROJECT MANAGEMENT, INC.

User Story Cards - Back

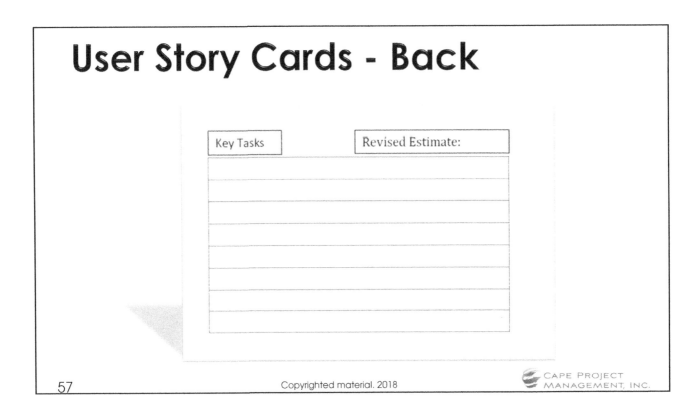

Copyrighted material. 2018 CAPE PROJECT MANAGEMENT, INC.

How detailed should a User Story be?

- Detailed enough...
- User stories should only provide enough detail to make a reasonably low risk estimate of how long the story will take to implement. When the time comes to implement the story developers will go to the customer and receive a detailed description of the requirements face-to-face.

http://www.extremeprogramming.org/rules/userstories.html

Copyrighted material. 2018 CAPE PROJECT MANAGEMENT, INC.

Why use User Stories?

- Keep the focus on expressing business value
- Avoids introducing detail too early that would prevent design options and inappropriately lock developers into one solution
- Avoids the appearance of false completeness and clarity
- Invites negotiation and movement in the backlog
- Leaves the technical functions to the architect, developers, testers, and so on

Note: Certain technical User Stories do not lend themselves to this format

59   Copyrighted material. 2018   CAPE PROJECT MANAGEMENT, INC.

Requirements vs. User stories

Requirements:

3.4) The Product needs to have an engine

3.5) The Product needs to have 4 wheels

    3.5.1) The Product needs to have rubber tires

3.6) The Product needs to have steering and acceleration

3.7) The Product needs to have a frame of steel

What are you thinking of?

60   Copyrighted material. 2018   CAPE PROJECT MANAGEMENT, INC.

Requirements vs. User stories[1]

User story:
As a gardener, I want an tool that allows me to mow my lawn faster and easier than with my current hand mower.

The team will have ask additional questions like :
- How big is your lawn ?
- What did you mean by "faster" and "easier?"

Acceptance criteria:
- I want to be able to mow 1 acre in 30 minutes
- I want to sit comfortably.

61

CAPE PROJECT
MANAGEMENT, INC.

Writing Stories

▸ Good stories are:
- Independent
- Negotiable
- Valuable to users or customers
- Estimable
- Small
- Testable (INVEST)

62

CAPE PROJECT
MANAGEMENT, INC.

Independent

- Stories that depend on other stories are difficult to prioritize and estimate
- Dependent Story:
  - As a user, I want to be able to log in and change my password
- Independent Stories
  - As a user, I want to be able to log in
  - As a user, I want the ability to change my password

Negotiable

- Story cards serve as reminders not contracts
- Details need to be fleshed out in conversation
- Story cards should have a phrase or sentence to serve as reminder to have conversation & notes about conversation

Valuable

- ▸ Both to people using the software and paying for the software
- ▸ Avoid stories valued only by developers (make the benefits to customers/users apparent for these stories)
- ▸ Example
  - ◦ "All connections to the database are through a connection pool" could be rewritten as "Up to 50 users should be able to use the application with a 5-user database license"

  CAPE PROJECT MANAGEMENT, INC.

Estimable

- ▸ 3 common reasons why a story might not be estimable
- ▸ Not enough information or team lacks domain knowledge
  - ◦ Get details from customer
- ▸ New technology or not enough knowledge in the team
  - ◦ Perform spike to explore technology
- ▸ Story is too big
  - ◦ Split the story into smaller ones

  CAPE PROJECT MANAGEMENT, INC.

Spikes

- ▸ Spikes, an invention of XP, are a special type of User Story used to drive out risk and uncertainty.
- ▸ Spikes may be used for basic research to familiarize the team with a new technology or domain.
- ▸ They are time-boxed to prevent excess analysis.
- ▸ Spikes may be used for estimating features in the next Sprint

  CAPE PROJECT MANAGEMENT, INC.

Small

- ▸ Small enough to use in planning
- ▸ Split Compound or Complex Stories
  - ◦ Conversations may reveal multiple stories
  - ◦ Split along Create/Replace/Update/Delete (CRUD)
  - ◦ Split along data boundaries
  - ◦ Use spikes to analyze complexity
- ▸ Combine too small stories
  - ◦ If a story is too small, it will take more time to define and test than to develop

  CAPE PROJECT MANAGEMENT, INC.

Vertical Slices for Splitting

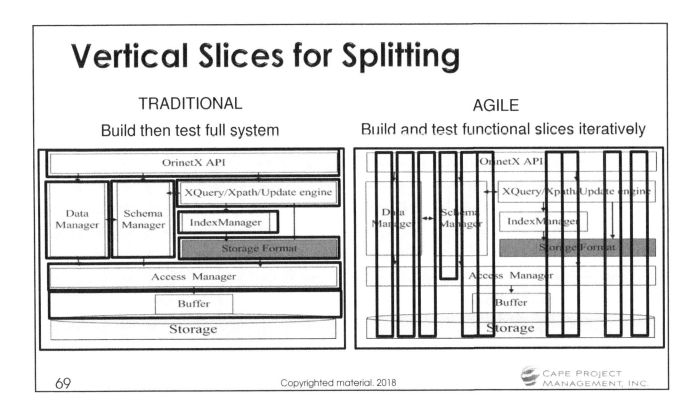

TRADITIONAL

Build then test full system

AGILE

Build and test functional slices iteratively

CAPE PROJECT
MANAGEMENT, INC.

Business Driven Approach to Splitting

Pattern	Before	After
CRUD Create / Read / Update / Delete	As a customer, I can manage my account	... sign up for an account ... view my account settings ... edit my account settings ... I cancel my account
Workflow	As a user, I want to use a check-out cart so that I can buy selected items	... enter my home and shipping addresses in checkout ... see the shipping costs calculated for my shipping address ... get an itemized view of all charges before I submit
Business Rules	As a user, I want to pay by online	... to pay by Mastercard ... to pay by Visa ... to pay by PayPal ... Investigate Bitcoin processing (Spike)
Screens	As a user I want to update my profile	... to update my billing information ... to update my contact information ... to change my password
Complexity	As a user I can search for products	... I can use a one word search for products ... I can use multiple words to search for products ... I can search with missplelled words

CAPE PROJECT
MANAGEMENT, INC.

DISCUSSION

How would you split these stories?
As a faculty member I want to search for a student.

As a student I want to pay online.

As An administrator I want to enter free text on screen.

Copyrighted material. 2018

Testable

- ▸ Can't tell if story is "done" without tests
- ▸ Aim for most tests to be automated
- ▸ Include Acceptance Criteria as part of the User Story

Copyrighted material. 2018

Acceptance Criteria

- ▸ Acceptance criteria define the boundaries of a User Story, and are used to confirm when a story is completed and working as intended.
- ▸ The tests are written before development
- ▸ They are ideally created by the Product Owner
- ▸ Does not replace unit tests
- ▸ Often written on the back of the User Story card

73   Copyrighted material. 2018    CAPE PROJECT MANAGEMENT, INC.

Writing Acceptance Tests

As a student, I want shopping cart functionality to easily pay tuition online.

Acceptance Criteria

- ▸ Student information is retained in a database
- ▸ Payment can be made via credit card, debit card, or PayPal
- ▸ An acknowledgment email is sent to the student after completing the transaction

74   Copyrighted material. 2018    CAPE PROJECT MANAGEMENT, INC.

Why use Acceptance Tests?

▸ They get the team to think through how a feature or piece of functionality will work from the user's perspective
▸ They remove ambiguity from requirements
▸ They form the tests that will confirm that a feature or piece of functionality is working and complete.

Write Stories by Role

▸ Define Roles
▸ Brainstorm an initial set of user roles
▸ Organize the initial set
▸ Consolidate roles
▸ Refine the roles
▸ Prioritize by role

What to consider when defining roles

▸ Frequency with which user will use software
▸ User's level of expertise with domain
▸ User's general level of proficiency with computers and software
▸ User's level of proficiency with this software
▸ User's general goal for using software

  CAPE PROJECT MANAGEMENT, INC.

GROUP EXERCISE

Exercise 4
Evaluate Stories

  CAPE PROJECT MANAGEMENT, INC.

User Story Examples: LMS Project

Theme 1: Document Management and Editing		Good/Bad
As a Faculty Member, I want...	assignments submitted via the LMS to be searched for direct quotes, so that I can identify students and work with plagiarism.	
As a Faculty Member, I want...	the first release to be in 4 months so that I can use it in the Fall semester	
As a Faculty Member, I want...	to download completed assignments directly to my computer, so that I can view files outside the LMS.	
As a Faculty Member, I want...	to ensure the Helvetica is part of the font set since it is the most readable heading font	
As a Student, I want...	to upload my completed assignments in less than 10 seconds	
As a Student, I want...	to upload content to the LMS as a PDF, so I can protect my content from editing.	
As a Student, I want...	to export the content of a discussion, so that I can view, edit and save in a word processing application on my desktop.	
Theme 2: Assessment & Grading		
As a Faculty Member, I want...	to import exams/assessments and exam questions from external sources (e.g. as MS-Word documents), so that I don't have to reenter them in the LMS.	
As a Faculty Member, I want...	I want to save my grades to f:/grades/instructors/ so that I can review them when I am not online	
As a Faculty Member, I want...	to calculate grades based on weighted averages, so that students always know their standing in the course.	
As a Faculty Member, I want...	to allow individual students to view individual grades, so that students can see their grades per assignment.	
As a Faculty Member, I want...	to export grades as a .xlsx file so that I can read and manipulate them in Excel 2010	
As a Student, I want to...	the option of showing everyone's grades in the class anonymously, so that students can compare their grades with the rest of the class.	
As a Student, I want to...	view all of my grades across all courses, so I do not need to enter each course.	
As a Student, I want to...	I want to be able to provide access to my parents to view my grades	

Gathering stories

▸ Trawl – Don't "Elicit" or "Capture"
▸ New metaphor for gathering stories
  ◦ Different sized nets for different sized stories
  ◦ Not all requirements are worth catching
  ◦ Requirements change, mature and some die
  ◦ You won't catch them all
  ◦ You will likely catch some debris
  ◦ Skill is required

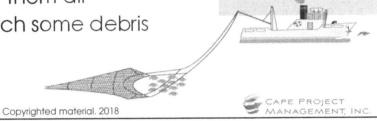

Copyrighted material. 2018

CAPE PROJECT
MANAGEMENT, INC.

Different "Nets"

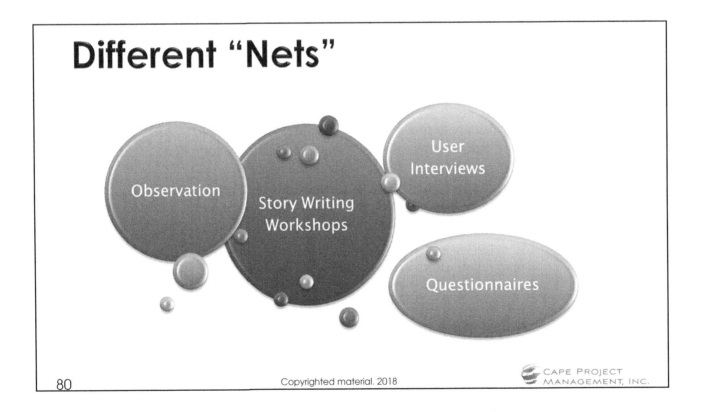

Copyrighted material. 2018

CAPE PROJECT
MANAGEMENT, INC.

Story-Writing Workshops

- ‣ Begin with vision, roadmap and release plan review
- ‣ Write as many stories as possible within a timebox – similar to brainstorming
- ‣ Involves stakeholders and Scrum Team
- ‣ Combine with low-fidelity prototyping or story boarding
- ‣ Ask questions that will help identify new stories:
  - ◦ What will user likely do next?
  - ◦ What mistakes could they make?
  - ◦ What could confuse them?
  - ◦ What additional information might they need?
- ‣ This workshop does not prioritize and estimate the user stories but solely identifies requirements.

Mike Cohn, User Stories Applied

81   Copyrighted material. 2018

GROUP EXERCISE

Exercise 5
Story Writing Workshop

82   Copyrighted material. 2018

Priority: Size:

As a:

I want to:(what)

So that: (why)

 CAPE PROJECT
MANAGEMENT, INC.

User Story Template

Priority: Size:

As a:

I want to:(what)

So that: (why)

CAPE PROJECT
MANAGEMENT, INC.

User Story Template

Product Backlog

As a	I want	Must Should Could Won't	T-Shirt Size XS=1 S=2 M=4 L=8 XL=16	Sprint
Faculty Member	assignments submitted via the LMS to be searched for direct quotes, so that I can identify students and work with plagiarism.	S	4	3

When is a User Story Ready?

▸ A story is **clear** if all Scrum team members have a shared understanding of what it means.
▸ An item is **testable** if there is an effective way to determine if the functionality works as expected. Acceptance criteria exists ensure that each story can be tested, typically there are three to five acceptance criteria per User Story.
▸ A story is **feasible** if it can be completed in one Sprint, according to the definition of done.
▸ **Ready** stories are the output of the product backlog refinement work.

CAPE PROJECT MANAGEMENT, INC.

Example Definition of "Ready"

▸ Story meets the criteria of INVEST
▸ Story traceable to source document (where appropriate)
▸ Acceptance criteria defined
▸ Size estimated by delivery team
▸ User experience included (where appropriate)
▸ Performance criteria identified (where appropriate)
▸ Person who will accept the User Story is identified
▸ Team has a good idea about how to demo the User Story

CAPE PROJECT MANAGEMENT, INC.

GROUP EXERCISE

Exercise 6
Peer Review

85

The Definition of Done?

"The Definition of Done (DoD) as a tool for bringing transparency to the work a Scrum Team is performing. It is related more to the quality of a product, rather than its functionality." ~Scrum Guide

- Defined by Product Owner and Team and updated every Sprint
- Considerations
  - Quality Metrics
  - Coding standards
  - Test coverage
  - Integration testing
  - Documented (just enough)
- Risks of unclear definition
  - Inaccurate Velocity
  - Technical debt
- 0/100% Rule

Done-Done

- Story is production ready
- There are enough features for it to be useful to users
- Integrated with other teams

https://www.scrum.org/Resources/Scrum-Glossary/Definition-of-Done

86

Good Enough Artifacts

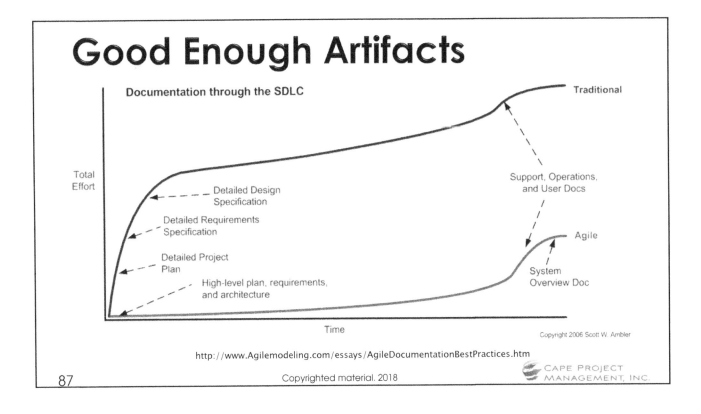

Copyrighted material. 2018

Challenges of Traditional Testing

▸ Large volumes of manual test activities slow down delivery.

▸ Teams put off testing until the end of projects, squeezing it in the process.

▸ Late-breaking defects can derail projects.

▸ Developers only see the results of poor quality in retrospect, when the consequences of their actions are harder and more costly to fix.

Copyrighted material. 2018

Benefits of Agile Testing

▸ On-going feedback to developers allows testers to ask the right questions at the right time.

▸ Early identification of dependencies, technical or testing challenges and roadblocks.

▸ Embraces change as a healthy and real part of software development.

▸ Team collaboration helps everyone work together toward a common goal.

▸ Quality comes first because final acceptance criteria are established prior to the work beginning.

89
CAPE PROJECT
MANAGEMENT, INC.

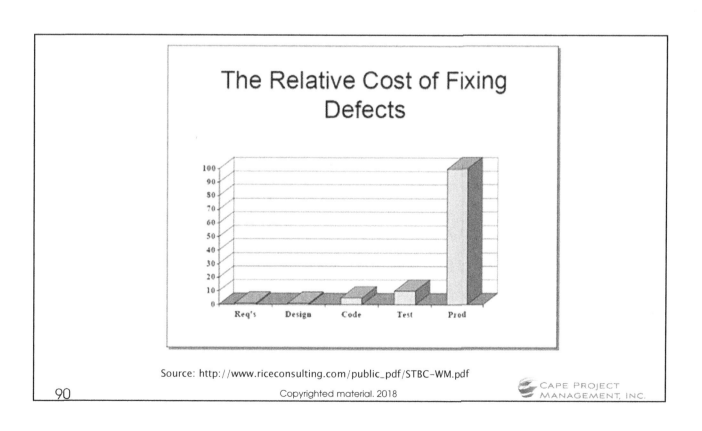

Source: http://www.riceconsulting.com/public_pdf/STBC-WM.pdf

90
CAPE PROJECT
MANAGEMENT, INC.

Shift Testing Left

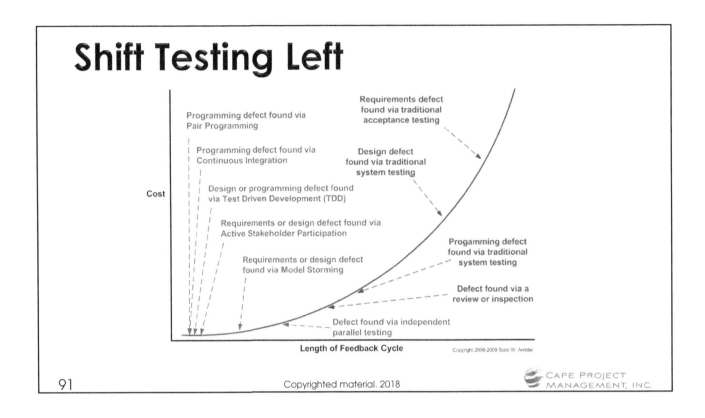

CAPE PROJECT
MANAGEMENT, INC.

Definition of Done

Example
- All code peer reviewed
- Compliant with coding standards
- Static testing with 0 errors and 0 warnings
- Dynamic testing – no memory leaks
- All code checked in to Subversion prod branch
- 80% code coverage – unit testing
- Zero known bugs
- Acceptance tests verified by QA on clean system
- Acceptance tests verified by Product Owner or proxy

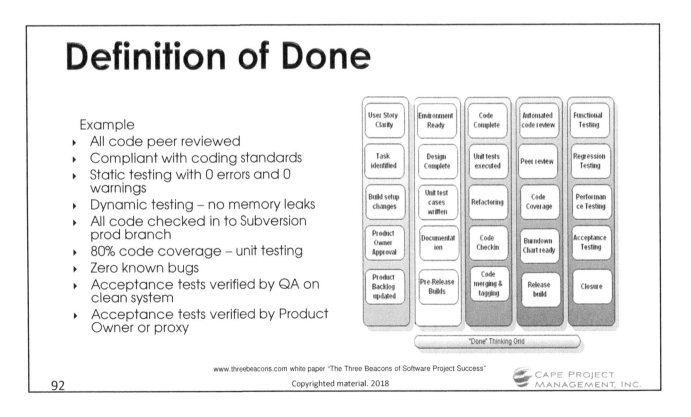

www.threebeacons.com white paper "The Three Beacons of Software Project Success"

CAPE PROJECT
MANAGEMENT, INC.

Activity: Definition on Done

Directions:
1. Return to your groups that developed the User Stories for the Case Study
2. Define done using the suggestions on the slides
3. Make sure some form of acceptance testing included
4. List the suggestions as if you would be posting this sheet on a war room wall

Definition of Done:

GROUP EXERCISE

Exercise 7
Define Done

CAPE PROJECT
MANAGEMENT, INC.

The Evolution of a User Story

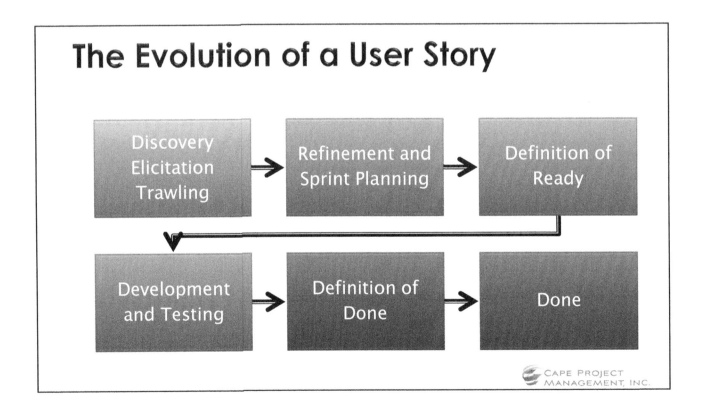

Additional Agile Requirements Techniques

Personas
Technical Requirements
Wireframes & Story boards
Agile Use Cases

CAPE PROJECT
MANAGEMENT, INC.

Personas

▸ Archetypal users of an application
▸ Fictitious but based upon knowledge of real users
▸ Help guide the functionality and design
▸ More accurate user stories can be written using personas

▸ As a user, I want to add a calendar entry
  ◦ As an admin, I want to create a calendar entry for an executive
  ◦ As an executive, I want to create a calendar entry for myself

CAPE PROJECT
MANAGEMENT, INC.

Persona Components

‣ Personal profile
‣ Experience
‣ Personal goals
‣ Professional goals

CAPE PROJECT
MANAGEMENT, INC.

Persona Example

‣ Jim is 50 years old and works as a mechanic with a company offering road service to customers when their car breaks down. He has worked in the job for the past 10 years and knows it well. Many of the younger mechanics ask Jim for advice. He always knows the answer to tricky mechanical problems.
‣ He is getting a new computer installed in his van. He doesn't own a computer, and he is a little intimidated by this type of technology.
‣ He is very nervous that he is going to look stupid if he can't figure it out.

What should you consider when building this system?

CAPE PROJECT
MANAGEMENT, INC.

Activity: Create an Extreme Persona

Directions:

1. Pick one of the following applications or an internal application and create an Extreme Persona for supporting the requirements process.
   - Exam tool for taking the Scrum Master Certification exam
   - Self-service application for ordering dentures online
   - A simulation software to teach first-time drivers
2. Create a profile below.
3. Be prepared to share your answers with the class.

Personal profile	

Activity

Exercise 8
Create an extreme persona

99   Copyrighted material. 2018

Technical Requirements

▸ Written by development team, architect, tech lead

▸ Don't have to be written as User Stories

▸ Often part of the Definition of Done

▸ Non-Functional Requirements (NFRs) should be part of the Acceptance Criteria

100   Copyrighted material. 2018

Technical Requirements in DoD

▸ All code must be peer reviewed within 4 hours of check-in.

▸ If a change is made to the web services interface, the change must be documented on the official web services api wiki page.

▸ All code must have automated testing that is consistent with the "Automated Testing Guidelines"

Copyrighted material. 2018  CAPE PROJECT MANAGEMENT, INC.

NFRs in Acceptance Criteria

Requirement type	Example
Performance	• Any interaction between the user and the system should not exceed 2 seconds. • The system should receive updated student information every 15 minutes.
Security	• Only direct managers can see personnel records of staff • Only students and bursar's office can see payment information
Cultural & Political	• The system should be able to distinguish between United States and European currency • The system shall comply with industry privacy standards.

Copyrighted material. 2018 CAPE PROJECT MANAGEMENT, INC.

Prioritizing Technical Requirements

▸ Projects have to balance delivering features along with doing all the important behind-the-scenes work.

▸ Leaving non-functional development until very late in the project has two major problems:
  1. It costs more
  2. It creates project risks that can lead to project problems

103

Wireframes

▸ "User Stories seek to combine the strengths of written and verbal communication, where possible supported by a **picture**."

▸ Low-fidelity (prototype)

▸ Black and white

▸ Combined to create a story board – sequence of screens

▸ Iteratively improved

▸ Validates design and understanding of user stories

104

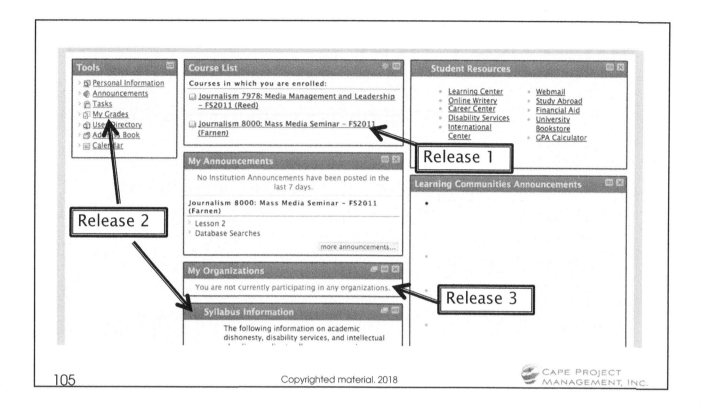

CAPE PROJECT
MANAGEMENT, INC.

Use Cases versus User Story

A Use Case is:	A User Story is:
<ul><li>the specification of a set of actions</li><li>performed by a system</li><li>yields an observable result of value for one or more actors of the system.</li></ul>	<ul><li>a simple, clear, brief description</li><li>expressing a user's goal for using the system under development</li><li>to deliver business value</li></ul>

- Both methods are focusing on users and values to the users
- Each has its own challenges
- Use cases are often used for new products and user stories for incremental releases

CAPE PROJECT
MANAGEMENT, INC.

Agile Use Cases

▸ Write just enough content to plan the needed horizon
  ◦ Project and release planning-> use briefs.
  ◦ Sprint planning-> Full use case and extension handling.
▸ Just barely beat the programmers to the extension handling decisions
▸ Write just enough content for the team to understand.
▸ Show the Use Cases to stakeholders for feedback

Copyrighted material. 2018  CAPE PROJECT MANAGEMENT, INC.

Use Case Briefs

▸ Write briefs to estimate & plan project.

Actor	Goal	Brief Description
Student	Register for Courses On–line	Student searches for course by major, identifies available timeslots, registers and receives confirmation

▸ Write full use cases just-in-time

Copyrighted material. 2018  CAPE PROJECT MANAGEMENT, INC.

Full Use Case

Course Enrollment

1. Student requests to create a schedule.
2. The system prepares a blank schedule form.
3. The system gets available courses from the Course Catalog System.
4. Student selects up to 4 primary and 2 alternate course offerings.
5. For each course, the system verifies that the Student has the necessary prerequisites, adds the Student to the course, marking Student as "enrolled" for that course in the schedule.
6. The Student indicates the schedule is complete, the system saves it.

Extensions:

1a. Student already has a schedule: System brings up the current version of the Student's schedule for editing instead of creating a new one.
1b. Current semester is closed and next semester is not yet open: System lets Student look at existing schedules, but not create new ones.
3a. Course Catalog System does not respond: The system notifies the Student and the use case ends.
5a. Course full or Student has not fulfilled all prerequisites: System disables selection of that course and notifies the Student

Guidelines for Agile Requirements

- Start with themes or epics
- Create user stories that meet the criteria of INVEST
- Include user roles in stories rather than saying "user"
- Don't rely solely on stories if they can be better expressed in other ways
- Size your story appropriately for the time frame it may be implemented in
- Ensure all completed stories meet a definition of "Done"

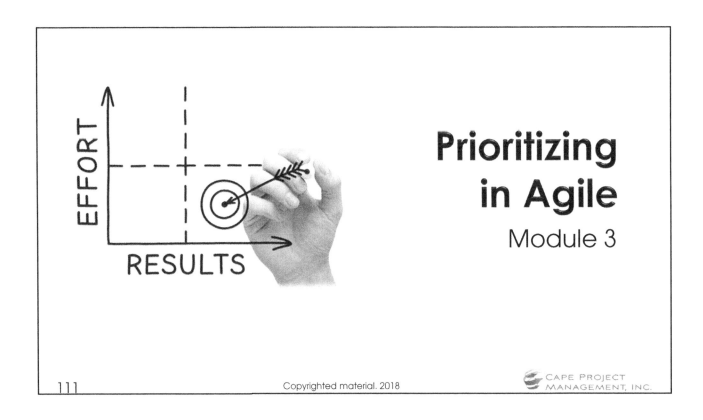

Prioritizing in Agile

Module 3

CAPE PROJECT
MANAGEMENT, INC.

Prioritize items in a backlog

- The Product Owner prioritizes the product backlog items
- The backlog is prioritized so that the most valuable items have the highest priorities
- Prioritization by Release translates to the Product Roadmap

CAPE PROJECT
MANAGEMENT, INC.

Agile Triangle

Value
- Meets or exceeds customer value expectations
- Value "chunks" are delivered in time-boxed releases

Quality
- Today's quality: Is the product reliable?
- Tomorrow's quality: Is the product adaptable to change?

Constraints
- Scope: all planned major value-generating capabilities are delivered.
- Cost: actual costs are within agreed to limits
- Schedule: actual schedule is within agreed to limits

113
Copyrighted material. 2018
CAPE PROJECT
MANAGEMENT, INC.

Focus on Value

The Traditional Iron Triangle

The Agile Triangle

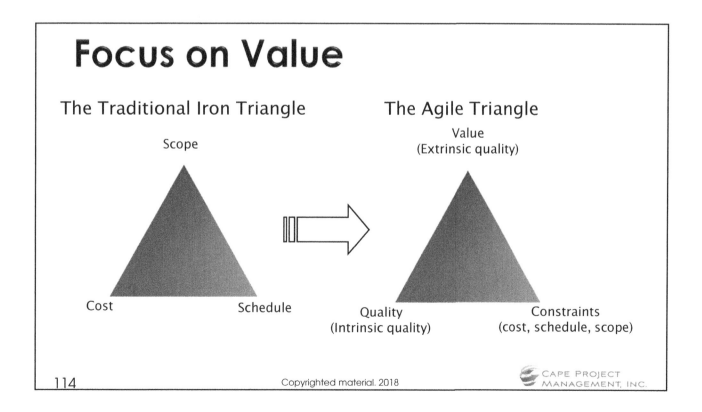

114
Copyrighted material. 2018
CAPE PROJECT
MANAGEMENT, INC.

Quality Defined

- Intrinsic Quality
  - All of the qualities that were built into the product: suitability, durability, reliability, uniformity, maintainability.
- Extrinsic Quality
  - Perceived quality
  - Value to the customer

Kelada, Joseph, *Integrating Reengineering with Total Quality*

115

Determining Value Quanitatively

- Return on investment (ROI)
- Net present value (NPV)
- Internal rate of return (IRR)
- Payback Period

116

Customer-Valued Prioritization Techniques

- ▸ Minimally marketable feature (MMF)
- ▸ Cumulative voting (the money game)
- ▸ MoSCoW prioritization
- ▸ Kano analysis
- ▸ Risk-based prioritization
- ▸ Weight Shortest Job First (WSJF)
- ▸ Relative Ranking
- ▸ Pareto analysis
- ▸ Kitchen Prioritization

117   Copyrighted material. 2018    CAPE PROJECT MANAGEMENT, INC.

Minimally Marketable Features (MMF)

- ▸ Identify the product's most desirable features
- ▸ Prioritize their value
- ▸ Plan your releases around the features
- ▸ Release the highest-value features first
- ▸ Collaborate on one feature at a time
- ▸ Perform releases as often as possible
- ▸ Can be related to user story approach via epics or themes

118   Copyrighted material. 2018    CAPE PROJECT MANAGEMENT, INC.

Cumulative Voting

▸ Hundred dollar method
▸ Give each stakeholder $100 in play money and they can "spend" it the requirements they want the most
▸ Can use points, stickers, etc.

119   Copyrighted material. 2018   CAPE PROJECT MANAGEMENT, INC.

MoSCoW Prioritization

Acronym	Description
M – MUST	Describes a requirement that must be satisfied in the final solution for the solution to be considered a success.
S – SHOULD	Represents a high-priority item that should be included in the solution if it is possible. This is often a critical requirement but one which can be satisfied in other ways if strictly necessary.
C – COULD	Describes a requirement which is considered desirable but not necessary. This will be included if time and resources permit.
W – WON'T	Represents a requirement that stakeholders have agreed will not be implemented in a given release, but may be considered for the future.

120   Copyrighted material. 2018   CAPE PROJECT MANAGEMENT, INC.

Kano Analysis

Need	Definition
Exciters/Delighters	Exceeds customer needs, and a "nice to have." Contributes 100% to positive customer satisfaction.
Performance/Linear	Competitive requirements that the customer "wants", typically an improvement over current system.
Basic/Baseline	Meets minimum requirements and is a "must have." If these features don't exist, the customer is dissatisfied.
Indifferent	Least important to the customer. They will likely return little or no business value.

121   Copyrighted material. 2018   CAPE PROJECT MANAGEMENT, INC.

Kano Analysis, Graphical

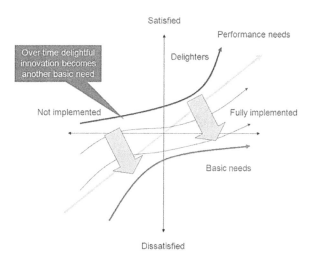

"Kano model showing transition over time" by Craig W Brown – Own work. Licensed under CC BY-SA 3.0 via Wikimedia Commons – Source: http://commons.wikimedia.org/wiki/File:Kano_model_showing_transition_over_time.png#/media/File:Kano_model_showing_transition_over_time.png

122   Copyrighted material. 2018   CAPE PROJECT MANAGEMENT, INC.

Risk-based Prioritization

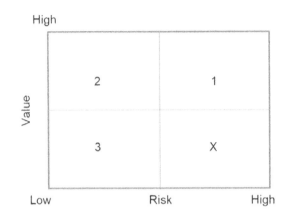

- ‣ Complete high-value, high-risk stories first
- ‣ Complete high-value, low-risk stories next
- ‣ Complete lower-value, low-risk stories next
- ‣ Avoid low-value, high-risk stories

123   Copyrighted material. 2018   CAPE PROJECT MANAGEMENT, INC.

Weighted Shortest Job First (WSJF)

- ‣ "Low Hanging Fruit" approach
- ‣ Assign a value to each story and divide that that by the length by the job size (points) determine a relative ranking.

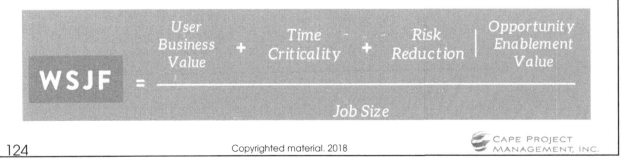

$$WSJF = \frac{User\ Business\ Value + Time\ Criticality + Risk\ Reduction\ |\ Opportunity\ Enablement\ Value}{Job\ Size}$$

124   Copyrighted material. 2018   CAPE PROJECT MANAGEMENT, INC.

Relative Prioritization/Ranking

- ▸ List all of the requirements
- ▸ Estimate the relative benefit
- ▸ Estimate the relative penalty
- ▸ Determine the total value
- ▸ Estimate the relative cost
- ▸ Estimate the relative degree
- ▸ Calculate priority number
- ▸ Sort the list of features by priority value (also called Value Pointing)

125   Copyrighted material. 2018   

Relative Prioritization

Feature	Relative Benefit	Relative Penalty	Total Value	Value %	Relative Cost	Cost %	Relative Risk	Risk %	Priority
Relative Weights:	2.0	1.0			1.0		0.5		
Print a material safety data sheet	2	4	8	5.2	1	2.7	1	3.0	1.22
Query status of a vendor order	5	3	13	8.4	2	5.4	1	3.0	1.21
Generate a Chemical Stockroom inventory report	9	7	25	16.1	5	13.5	3	9.1	0.89
See history of a specific chemical container	5	5	15	9.7	3	8.1	2	6.1	0.87
Search vendor catalogs for a specific chemical	9	8	26	16.8	3	8.1	8	24.2	0.83
Maintain a list of hazardous chemicals	3	9	15	9.7	3	8.1	4	12.1	0.68
Modify a pending chemical request	4	3	11	7.1	3	8.1	2	6.1	0.64
Generate an individual laboratory inventory report	6	2	14	9.0	4	10.8	3	9.1	0.59
Check training database for hazardous chemical training record	3	4	10	6.5	4	10.8	2	6.1	0.47
Import chemical structures from structure drawing tools	7	4	18	11.6	9	24.3	7	21.2	0.33
Totals	53	49	155	100.0	37	100.0	33	100.0	

Source: Karl Wiegers, *First Things First: Prioritizing Requirements*

126   Copyrighted material. 2018   

Pareto Analysis

- ▸ The 80/20 rule
- ▸ Which 20% of items will yield 80% of the business value?
- ▸ Used in backlog planning, prioritization, design considerations, etc.

Copyrighted material. 2018 CAPE PROJECT MANAGEMENT, INC.

Pareto Analysis, continued

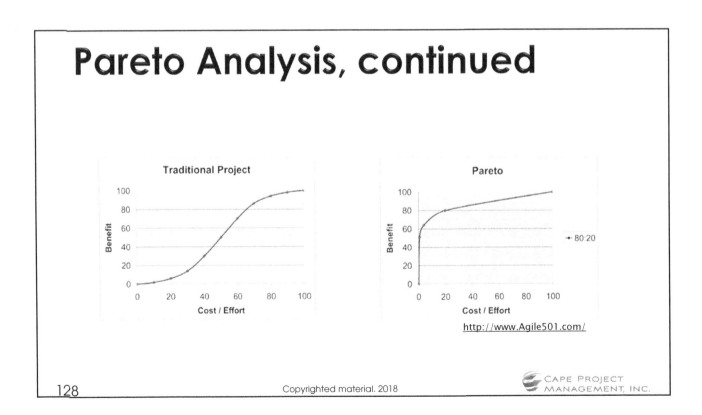

http://www.Agile501.com/

Copyrighted material. 2018 CAPE PROJECT MANAGEMENT, INC.

Kitchen Prioritization

- **Front Burner**: Stories that the Team has agreed to do in the current Sprint
- **Back Burner:** High priority, well-defined Stories that are being made actionable so that they will be ready for the next Sprint Planning – created during backlog grooming
- **Fridge:** Items (Stories or Epics) that are in scope for the Release, but are not yet ready to be taken to Sprint Planning either due to prioritization or readiness
- **Freezer:** Items that are out of the scope of the Release
- **Inbox:** Items that have not yet been prioritized into a bucket (or, in this case, an appliance)
- **Done:** Stories that have been completed

https://uploads.strikinglycdn.com/files/56888/5b9f15b3-7010-4f9a-b591-58e5b69c6463/Scrum-101-A-Pocket-Guide.pdf

 CAPE PROJECT MANAGEMENT, INC.

GROUP EXERCISE

Exercise 9
Prioritize User Stories

  CAPE PROJECT MANAGEMENT, INC.

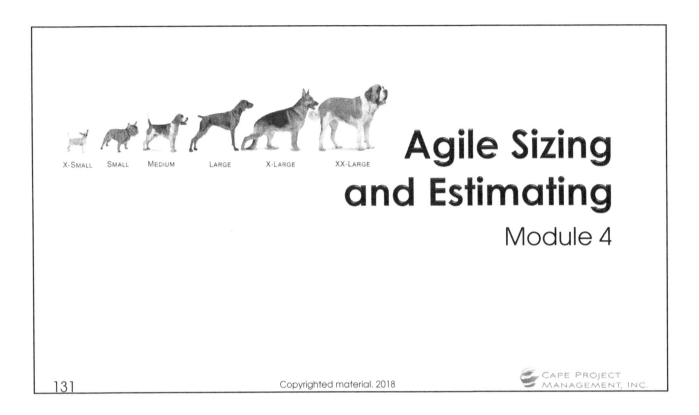

131

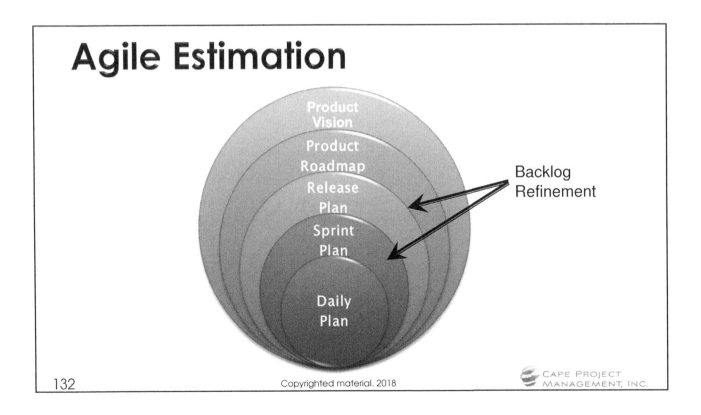

132

Reviewing Stories in Backlog Refinement

Product Owner
▸ Orders and reviews backlog
▸ Makes priority adjustments based on feedback from delivery team
▸ Ensures that higher priority items have more detail

Delivery Team
▸ Asks questions
▸ Understands the objective, not just the desired features
  ◦ Key to flexibility and risk management
▸ Breaks large stories (Epics) into smaller stories
▸ Estimates Story Sizes

133

CAPE PROJECT MANAGEMENT, INC.

Agile Sizing and Estimating

▸ Assumes all traditional estimates are inaccurate, essentially we are guessing
▸ Focuses on rapid/order of magnitude estimating
▸ There are many Agile Estimating Tools and Techniques
▸ Occurs during backlog refinement and Sprint planning

134

CAPE PROJECT MANAGEMENT, INC.

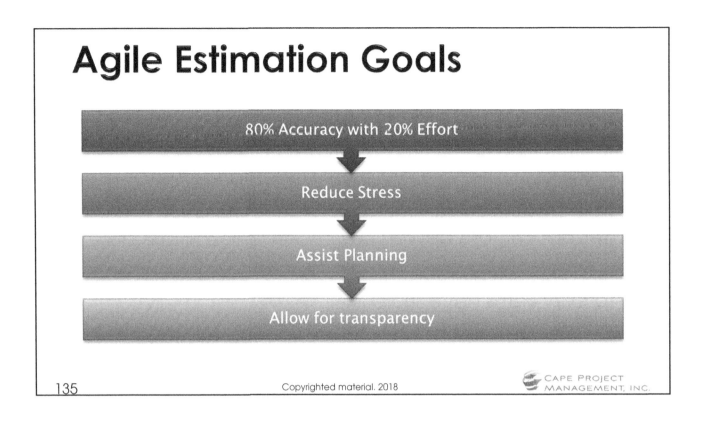

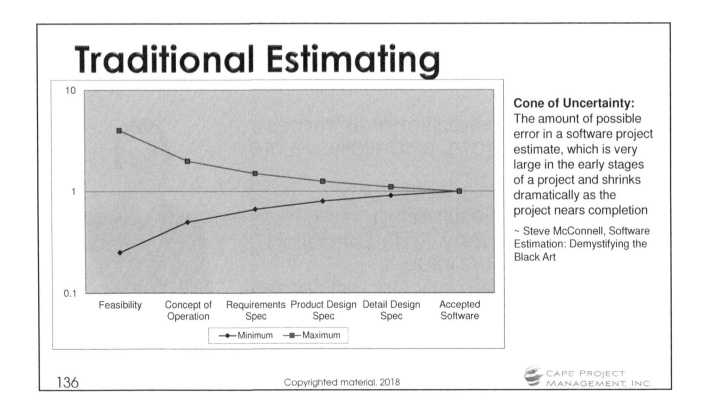

Agile Estimating Techniques

- Story points
- Planning poker
- T-Shirt Sizes
- Fibonacci Sequence
- Swimlane Sizing

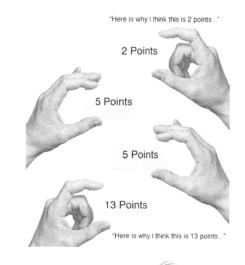

Copyrighted material. 2018

Story Points

- The "bigness" of a task
- Influenced by:
  - How hard it is
  - How much of it there is
- Relative values are what is important:
  - A login screen is a 2.
  - A search feature is an 8.
- Points are unit-less

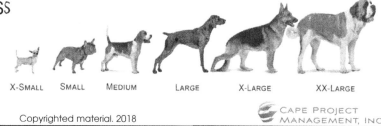

Copyrighted material. 2018

Benchmarking

Select a benchmark story or stories	Estimate each additional story by comparing it to the benchmark	If a User Story is bigger than an iteration or difficult to size use a very large number

If multiple teams are working on the same backlog, they need the same benchmarks.

CAPE PROJECT
MANAGEMENT, INC.

Planning Poker

1. Each team member is given a deck of cards
2. Product-Owner reads a story
3. The story is briefly discussed, questions answered etc.
4. Each team member secretly selects a card that is his or her estimate
5. Cards are presented to the group at the same time
6. Differences and outliers are discussed
7. Re-estimate until estimates converge

CAPE PROJECT
MANAGEMENT, INC.

T-Shirt Sizes

- Small, Medium, Large, X-Large, XX-Large
- A non-numerical approach is often easier for new teams
- Use cards to estimate
  - Similar to planning poker
- Assign values to each size, typically 1,2,4,8,16 story points

CAPE PROJECT MANAGEMENT, INC.

Fibonacci Sequence

- 0 1 1 2 3 5 8 13 21 34 55...
- Provides more flexibility for unknown larger stories
- Limit the largest number
- Use cards to estimate
  - Similar to planning poker

CAPE PROJECT MANAGEMENT, INC.

Relative Estimating using Swimlanes

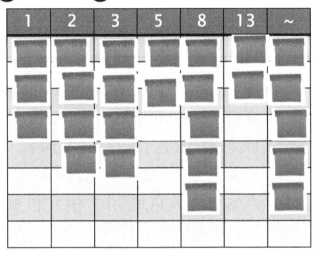

- ▸ Order each user story from easiest to hardest
- ▸ Group similar size stories together
- ▸ Leave a column for Epics
- ▸ Label using Fibonacci last

http://theagilepirate.net/archives/109

143

Avoid "Anchoring"

- ▸ Anchoring is a where the estimates of individuals are biased based on irrelevant information or strong personalities
- ▸ As a result, members will subconsciously use the given estimate as an anchor.
- ▸ To avoid this, the Scrum Master should instruct the team to estimate for themselves.
- ▸ Team members should reveal at the same time.

▸ 144

Combining Test and Development Estimates

- ▸ The total effort of the team is include the estimate
- ▸ Includes everything that meets the Definition of Done, e.g. unit testing, automated testing, regression, UAT, etc.
- ▸ Assume that there could be cross functional support
- ▸ Avoid Scrummerfall

145

CAPE PROJECT
MANAGEMENT, INC.

GROUP EXERCISE

Exercise 10
Estimate User Stories

146

CAPE PROJECT
MANAGEMENT, INC.

Sprint Planning

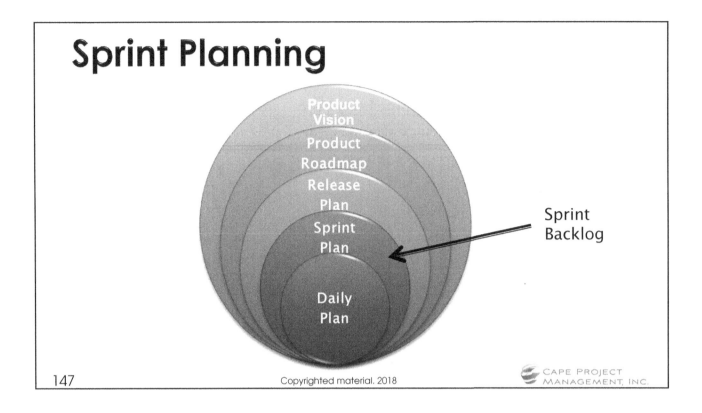

Sprint
Backlog

Sprint Planning

▸ The Development Team works with the Product owner to select those items that meet the Sprint Goal and will fit in a Sprint
▸ Based upon a refined Product Backlog
  ◦ Prioritized Stories
  ◦ Estimated Stories
▸ Sprint Backlog is created based upon story size, priority and velocity
▸ The Sprint Backlog is emergent and will evolve during the Sprint to meet the Sprint goal

Reviewing Stories

- Product Owner
  - Explain the Sprint objective
  - Present the User Stories which will meet the objective
  - Make priority adjustments based on feedback from delivery team
- Delivery Team
  - Ask Questions
  - Understand the objective, not just the desired features
  - Collaborates with the Product Owner to create the Sprint Goal

149   Copyrighted material. 2018   CAPE PROJECT MANAGEMENT, INC.

The Commitment (Forecast)

- By the end of the Sprint Planning, the Development Team should be able to explain to the Product Owner and Scrum Master how it intends to work as a self-organizing team to accomplish the Sprint Goal and create the anticipated Increment. ~Scrum Guide
- Drive agreement with a fist of five
  - This is the best idea possible
  - The only thing wrong with this idea is that it wasn't mine
  - I can support this idea
  - I'm uneasy about this and think we need to talk it out some more
  - Let's continue discussing this idea in the parking lot

150   Copyrighted material. 2018   CAPE PROJECT MANAGEMENT, INC.

Daily Planning

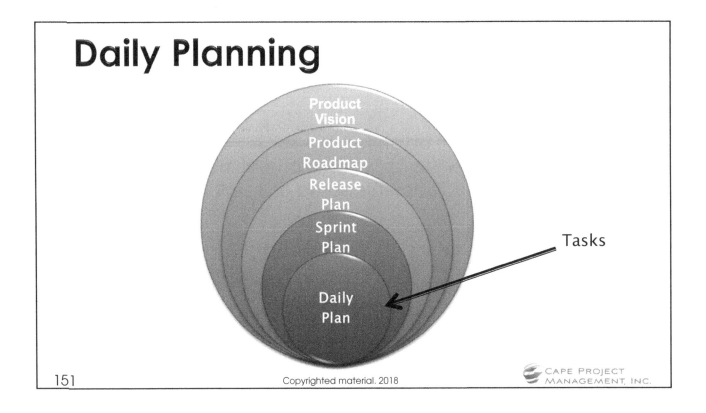

Tasks

CAPE PROJECT
MANAGEMENT, INC.

Define Tasks

▸ Through conversation among the team, define tasks
  ◦ Don't make task too granular (don't do 10 minute tasks)
  ◦ Don't make task too large (1 sprint length)
▸ Team members sign up for tasks, they are not assigned
▸ Any team member can add, delete, or change tasks, they often emerge during the Sprint

CAPE PROJECT
MANAGEMENT, INC.

Create User Story Tasks

User Story	Tasks
As a student, I want to be able to log in to the system	Design the…
	Meet with customer
	Design the UI
	Code and Unit Test the..
	Automate Tests…
As a faculty member, I want to update my contact information	Copy admin profile
	Design solution to..
	Validate Workflow
	Code the..
	Automate tests..

CAPE PROJECT
MANAGEMENT, INC.

Avoid Mini-Waterfall

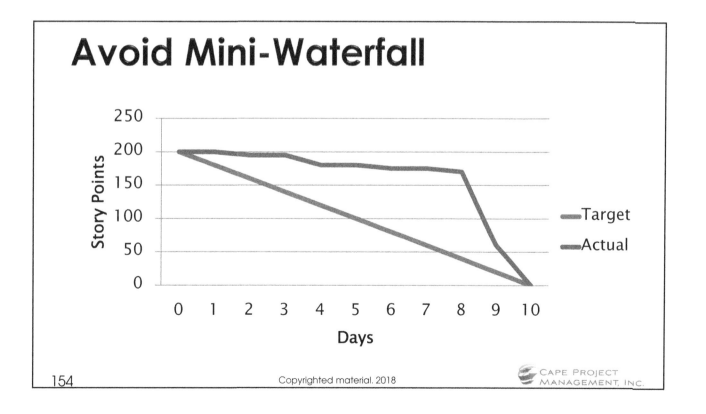

CAPE PROJECT
MANAGEMENT, INC.

Team Swarm (or Swarming)

- Working on one or more stories until they are done
- Each story has a "TeamLet"
- Each TeamLet has:
  - A **Coordinator** who is in charge of the story and stays with it until it is complete
  - A **Swarmer(s)** brings their expertise to the story. A Swarmer may be on multiple TeamLets.

CAPE PROJECT
MANAGEMENT, INC.

GROUP EXERCISE

Exercise 11
Task Definition

CAPE PROJECT
MANAGEMENT, INC.

An Example Checklist for Product Owners

Lare Lekman | Revised in November 2013 | productownerchecklist.org

Product Vision

☐ I have a product vision (created with customers, end users, and investors, when possible)

☐ I can answer to questions about the product vision and business model in a concise and motivating way

☐ I have a short tagline for the product vision, for example "1,000 songs in your pocket" (iPod in 2001), to communicate the essence and value of the product release.

Stakeholders

☐ I understand the needs of my stakeholders (for example customers, end users, and investors)

☐ I communicate regularly with my stakeholders to understand their needs and to manage their expectations

☐ I can answer to questions about how each product backlog item will generate value for the stakeholders

☐ I am motivated to work as a Product Owner, and make sure I have the stakeholders' mandate and trust

☐ My forecasts to stakeholders are based on development team's measured velocity or throughput

Product Backlog

☐ I have a product backlog

☐ I have a mandate to make decisions about the product backlog

☐ I update the product backlog at least before each sprint planning meeting

☐ The product backlog items are ordered (based on value, risk, work estimates, dependencies, etc.)

☐ The product backlog items are clearly expressed and more detailed towards the top

☐ The product backlog is accessible to all scrum team members

☐ I regularly refine the product backlog to make the top of it actionable for the next sprint (or release) planning meeting. The Scrum Team decides how and when refinement is done.

Development Team

☐ I am available to my developers during the sprint to clarify requirements

☐ I protect my development team from anyone who tries to change the sprint's product backlog items

☐ There is only one Product Owner who chooses the product backlog items and refines them with the development team. Otherwise, developers do not know who to listen.

☐ I motivate my development team by occasionally describing my product vision, including the planned benefits and impacts of the next product release or increment.

☐ I motivate and train my developers by involving them in writing and analyzing user stories, when possible (thus also reducing my own work).

☐ I trust my Scrum team's development capabilities. If not, I will try and build trust by offering them training, recruiting, better communication, personnel changes, etc.

☐ My Scrum team trusts my business domain and end user knowledge. If not, I will try and build trust by improving my own and the Scrum team's business and end user understanding.

☐ I have a similar understanding of the Definition of Done with the Scrum team

Scrum Master

☐ A Scrum Master is appointed (preferably by the development team, when possible)

☐ I have a good understanding and trust with my Scrum Master. If not, I work together with my Scrum Master to improve our cooperation.

Scrum Events

☐ I participate in sprint planning meetings to select the product backlog items with the team

☐ I participate in sprint review meetings, give and gather constructive feedback, and verify which of the selected product backlog items fulfill their unique Acceptance Criteria and the general Definition of Done.

☐ I participate in retrospective meetings to observe and improve my own work as a Product Owner

☐ I work with my development team even on daily basis, when needed, to clarify the requirements, work on the design, and optimize the sprint's outcome.

☐ I have scheduled sprint events with Scrum Master (for example as repetitive calendar events)

My current Product Owner Score is _____ / 30 points

Product Owner Checklist

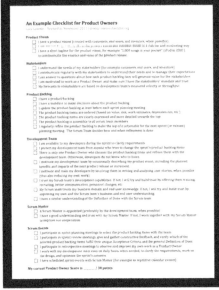

DISCUSSION

What did you learn that was useful?
What changes can you make immediately?
What changes require work that should planned?

Thank-You!

dan@CapeProjectManagement.com

Twitter: @scrumdan

CAPE PROJECT
MANAGEMENT, INC.

User Story References

1. Ralph, Paul (2015). "The Sensemaking-coevolution-implementation theory of software design". Science of Computer Programming. 101: 21–41. arXiv:1302.4061 . doi:10.1016/j.scico.2014.11.007.

2. "Origin of story card is a promise for a conversation : Alistair.Cockburn.us". alistair.cockburn.us. Retrieved 2017-08-16.

3. Beck, Kent (1999). "Embracing change with extreme programming". IEEE Computer. 32 (10): 70–77.

4. Ron Jeffries (August 30, 2001). "Essential XP: Card, Conversation, Confirmation".

5. https://www.agilealliance.org/glossary/role-feature/

6. Mishkin Berteig (2014-03-06). "User Stories and Story Splitting". Agile Advice. Retrieved 2017-02-23.

7. AntonyMarcano (2011-03-24). "Old Favourite: Feature Injection User Stories on a Business Value Theme". Antonymarcano.com. Retrieved 2017-02-23.

8. Weldemichael, Weldemichael. "User Story Template Advantages". Mountaingoatsoftware.com. Retrieved 2017-02-23.

9. "10 Tips for Writing Good User Stories". Romanpichler.com. Retrieved 2017-02-23.

10. Cowan, Alexander. "Your Best Agile User Story". Cowan+. Retrieved 29 April 2016.

11. Cohn, Mike. "User Stories". Mountain Goat Software. Retrieved 27 April2016.

12. Ralph, Paul; Mohanani, Rahul. "Is Requirements Engineering Inherently Counterproductive?". IEEE. doi:10.1109/TwinPeaks.2015.12.

13. "Limitations of user stories". Ferolen.com. April 15, 2008.

14. Patton, Jeff. "The new user story backlog is a map". Retrieved 17 May 2017.

15. Pichler, Roman. "10 Tips for Writing Good User Stories". Retrieved 29 July2014.

16. Cohn, Mike. "User Stories, Epics and Themes". Mountaingoatsoftware.com. Retrieved 26 September 2017.

17. Cockburn, Alistair. "Walking Skeleton". Retrieved 4 March 2013.

18. "Story Mapping". Agile Alliance. Retrieved 1 May 2016.

19. Cohn, Mike. "Project Advantages of User Stories as Requirements". Mountaingoatsoftware.com. Retrieved 26 September 2017.

20. Martin Fowler (18 August 2003). "UseCasesAndStories". Retrieved 26 September 2017.

CAPE PROJECT
MANAGEMENT, INC.

Appendix

WHAT IS A USER STORY?

A user story is an agile project management tool used to define product or system functionality and the associated benefit of the functionality. In an Agile environment, projects are commonly comprised of a large number of user stories representing various levels of system/product user. The user story describes the type of system/product user, what functionality they want, and why they want it (or why it's beneficial). The format of a user story is:

As a *<type of user>*, I want to *<feature/function>* so that *<reason/benefit>*.

The purpose of the user story is to encourage collaboration among the project team for each defined function of the system or product being developed. Agile project management places emphasis on collaboration rather than formal documentation. Because of this, each user story created by the team represents an opportunity for the team to collaborate, decide which user stories will be worked on in the next Sprint, further define the functionality (during Sprint planning), and accomplish the work.

While user stories represent a simplified approach to defining functionality, the challenge for the project team is developing user stories with the appropriate level of detail.

THE CHARACTERISTICS OF A USER STORY

All user stories should be developed with the expectation that once completed, the functionality defined in the user story will add value to the final product. If it does not add value to the finished product then it should be avoided.

Finding the appropriate level of detail for user stories is often a challenge for the team. User stories should be general enough to provide a description of the functionality and the benefit while also allowing for innovation and creativity for developing a solution. They should not be so detailed as to lock the team into only one way of accomplishing the solution.

In the creation of their user stories, many agile practitioners subscribe to the INVEST acronym created by Bill Wake which states that user stories should be:

Independent – user stories should not be sequential or locked into a specific order. The team should be able to develop the user stories in any sequence.

Negotiable – user stories should be flexible and without too much detail. Details will be added later through team collaboration.

Valuable – the user stories should add value to the final product.

Estimable – the team must be able to use the user stories to estimate/approximate work.

Small – large or vague user stories are difficult to estimate. User stories should be able to be designed, built, and tested within a single Sprint.

Testable – the user story should be able to be tested with some type of acceptance criteria or other test (even if it has not yet been defined)

Acceptance criteria, while not formally a part of the user story format, is a crucial component of user stories. As user stories evolve toward Sprint planning, the team should collaboratively discuss the acceptance criteria for satisfying each user story. Acceptance criteria are used by the team to understand when the intent of the user story has been met. Additionally, acceptance criteria are often used by the product/system testers to develop the acceptance tests for the user story.

Acceptance tests are developed to test the functionality of each user story. While an acceptance criteria ensures that a certain functionality is included in a Sprint, an acceptance test ensures that functionality performs as expected.

WHAT TO AVOID WHEN WRITING USER STORIES

User stories provide an effective tool to encourage communication and collaboration among the team. However, there are several common mistakes that teams make when developing their user stories which often reduce their effectiveness. Some of these mistakes include:

Too much detail – user stories should be broad enough to allow for flexibility and a collaborative effort to further define the user story during Sprint planning when the team agrees to incorporate it into the next Sprint. User stories with too much detail may lock the team into only one way to develop a solution which discourages innovation and creativity.

Lack of acceptance criteria – as user stories evolve, the team must discuss and capture acceptance criteria. Without acceptance criteria, the team will have no ability of knowing when they've satisfied the user story. Additionally, a lack of acceptance criteria will result in a lack of acceptance testing which hampers the team's ability to ensure functionality of the product performs as expected.

EXAMPLES OF USER STORIES: GOOD AND BAD

Below are examples of user stories which include too much detail, not enough detail, and an appropriate amount of detail.

Too Much Detail:

As an end user, I want the ability to access the human resource database to generate a staffing report with employee names, dates of birth, social security numbers, addresses, and telephone numbers so that I can periodically update the company's staffing contact list.

Note that the above example goes into listing details about what the report should include. Including these items in the user story may prevent or discourage the team from including other important content in reports that will be built. This level of detail should be defined later during Sprint planning.

Too Broad:

As an end user, I want access to the human resource database so that I can periodically update the company's staffing contact list.

Note that the above example mentions nothing about the ability to generate reports from the human resource database. Only access to the database is mentioned. By leaving out the key information about generating a report, the team might overlook this important functionality and only grant access to the database when the Sprint is performed.

Appropriate Level of Detail:
As an end user, I want to access the human resource database to generate reports so that I can periodically update the company's staffing contact list.

The above example ensures that when Sprint planning begins, the team can plan for both access and report generating while further defining what information the reports will consist of.

USER STORY WITH ACCEPTANCE CRITERIA AND ACCEPTANCE TESTING

Below is an example of a single user story with both the acceptance criteria and acceptance testing information included.

User Story:
As an end user, I want to access the human resource database to generate reports so that I can periodically update the company's staffing contact list.

Acceptance Criteria:
- Ability to gain access to human resource database
- Ability to generate a report which includes
  - Employee names
  - Dates of birth
  - Social security numbers
  - Addresses
  - Telephone numbers
- Ability to use report data to update staffing contact list

Acceptance Testing:
- Database is accessible internally but not from outside company firewall
- MS Access report can be generated from database based on query inputs
- MS Access report data can be exported to MS Excel spreadsheet
- Staffing contact list updates contain only most recent data from the database

THE PRODUCT BACKLOG

User Stories are captured in a Product Backlog. There are several characteristics of the product backlog, which are important to understand:
1) The product backlog is a living document – items are added, changed, and/or removed from the backlog throughout the entire duration of the project.
2) All backlog items should be estimated – this is done in the form of user points which measure the effort required to complete the backlog item (as opposed to hours or man-hours)

3) All backlog items should be prioritized – prioritization may be based on risks, benefits/value, costs, or estimates (story points) and ensures the most important items are completed first

4) All backlog items should add value to the project – if items are determined not to add value, they should be omitted from the backlog

5) Backlog items may have varying level of detail – as iterative sprint planning occurs and items are selected for the upcoming sprint, these items will often have a more granular level of detail than other items

Product Backlog for New Payroll System			
Task ID	**Story**	**Estimate**	**Priority**
4	As a user, I want to enter my work hours so I can make sure I get paid on time	5	1
2	As an administrator, I want to approve timesheets so employees get paid	4	2
3	As a user, I want to log in to the system so I can perform payroll functions	4	3
1	As a user, I want to log off of the system so no one can enter erroneous information in my account	4	4
6	As an administrator, I want to run consolidated payroll reports so I can provide a weekly status to senior management	10	5
5	As an administrator, I want the ability to create new accounts so we can add employees after they're hired	7	6
8	As a user, I want the ability to edit my timesheet so I can correct any mistakes	5	7
7	As an administrator, I want the ability to set automated reminders so employees will verify and sign their timesheets on time	9	8
9	As an administrator, I want the ability to archive timesheets so the organization can file them for audit and tax purposes	15	9

References: Mike Cohn, *User Stories Applied*

LMS Functionality User Stories

1 Document Management and Editing
As a Faculty Member, I want...

to access the same online document as other users, so that learners can edit documents collaboratively.

multiple authors to edit the same document throughout the LMS environment, yet each does not have to log in to the LMS multiple times or in to multiple systems.

assignments submitted via the LMS to be searched for direct quotes, so that I can identify students and work with plagiarism.

to download completed assignments directly to my computer, so that I can edit files outside the LMS.

content fidelity (characters, formatting) after uploading my documents to the LMS, so I can use a the Macintosh versions of word processing tools.

to edit and save documents in the LMS, so that I do not have to download the file to my local desktop.

the screen to return to the area I was working after I submit/save, so that I do not have to scroll back down to where I was working from the top of the page when it refreshes.

to include programming code in my assignments, so they do not interfere with the functionality of the LMS yet the syntax/format/characters remain accurate.

As a Student, I want...

printer friendly formats for the LMS interfaces/tools, so I can work off line without losing content, context or wasting paper.

to save content from the LMS as a PDF, so I can protect my content from editing.

to export the content of a discussion, so that I can view, edit and save in a word processing application on my desktop.

to access other online services offered by my campus (e.g. tutoring, bookstore, library), so I can get feedback about my work directly from within the LMS.

no limit on the length of text I can write within a message reply, so I can write my entire paper in the LMS.

2 Communications
As a Faculty Member, I want...

access to communications (e.g. IM, Chat, Forums, etc.) tools outside of their, or any, section, so that students can communicate across multiple sections.

to identify specific discussion forum posts, so that I can grade the student responses.

to be notified whenever a new message is posted to a discussion I am subscribed to, so that I don't have to enter the LMS to check for each topic's updates.

to view a new discussion board message independently and individually without affecting the status (e.g. read, new, unread) of other posted messages, so that I don't have to read all of the new messages in one session.

to use [move] discussion topics and threads from another section to any other, so that I do not have to manually copy and paste from one course to the next.

to search course email by date, author, group, keyword, course/section and other criteria, so that I can find emails based on a specific and single attribute.

integrate external (e.g. personal or campus) and course emails from the LMS, so that students can respond to e-mail sent to them from the course without having to log onto the course web site to respond.

to post announcements, so that they get the immediate attention of my students while in the LMS.

send my language students voice messages, announcements to my students, so they can hear proper pronunciation and inflection.

to send a voice (audio) email within the course, so it is accessible in the site by faculty and students.

to push notifications to students through the LMS using external communications channels (e.g. email, IM, SMS, etc.), so that I do not need to log into the LMS to update my class.

to push notifications to students through the LMS using external communications channels (e.g. email, IM, SMS, etc.), so that my students don't have to log into the LMS to receive important updates.

to automatically send a notification to students when their grades/activity fall below a standard I set, so that students can adjust their behavior in order to complete/pass the course.

to have a course discussion that occurs outside of each section, so that students can learn from one another's field experiences across multiple sections.

As a Student, I want to...

view in one place all classmates that have contributed to a project, document activity, so that I can see what has been done and by whom.

view all assignments and due dates for a course in one place, so that I can identify what I need to do and when across the course.

to be notified via communications channels outside of the LMS, so that I can be reminded about approaching, class start dates, assignment due dates and exam dates.

set notification attributes, so I can define the time, frequency and type of alerts that are sent to me.

to be notified whenever a new message is posted to a discussion I am subscribed to, so that I don't have to enter the LMS to check for each topic's updates.

see who else is online in my course, so I can communicate with classmates and faculty in real time.

see who else is online across the LMS, so I can communicate with classmates and faculty in real time.

audio and video based synchronous communications, so that I can keep up with the class discussions without typing.

sort discussion posts, so that I can view the thread of a discussion.

to view course updates in my RSS reader, so I do not have to be in the LMS to find out about updates.

to post profile information about me, so other students and faculty can know more about each other.

to see all discussions in one view, so I can open any active discussion from the same page.

the professor to be notified via channels outside of the LMS, so they know when a student sends and email to them.

access to communications (e.g. IM, Chat, Forums, etc.) tools outside of my, or any, section, so that I can communicate across multiple sections with other students.

As a Librarian, I want...

access to independent synchronous communication tools within the LMS, so that I can work with students independent of a their courses.

3 Assessment & Grading

As a Faculty Member, I want...

to import exams/assessments and exam questions from external sources (e.g. as MS-Word documents), so that I don't have to reenter them in the LMS.

to import grades from other sources/systems, so that I can calculate a final graded including work that may have been done and assessed in another tool.

to calculate grades based on weighted averages, so that students always know their standing in the course.

to allow individual students to view individual grades, so that students can see their grades per assignment.

to allow individual students to view their course grades throughout the term, so they can see their standing in the course.

to scale and resize the grade book, so that I can see all of the students grades for the semester in one view.

various grading methods, so that I can grade based on points or letter grades.

to create formulas, so that I can convert points to letter grades.

to export grades in standard and popular file/exchange formats, so I can use external applications to manage my grades.

to create multiple versions of the same exam, so that questions can be randomized

to create multiple versions of the same exam, so that multiple choice questions can be randomized.

to include private or public comments when grading a student's discussion post, so I do not have to email him/her separately.

to include private comments with all graded items, so I do not have to email students separately.

set up standardized grading criteria and standards, so I can score assignments subjectively related to learning objectives.

to associate/migrate grading criteria (rubrics, weights, formulas) with multiple sections, so I do not need to recreate them for each course/section.

to read a student's discussion posting, see the grading rubric and/or an email window at the same time, so I can write comments and calculate a grade while reading the postings.

to view the series of steps students undertake when solving calculation-based engineering/math problems, so I can assess problem solving.

a high-level math/scientific scripting language within all editors, so I can create text-based (not image-based) equations within the LMS.

to provide feed back and grades in voice threads, so that students can see comments and grades in the context of their work.

to set the time to finish a single test independently for individual students or groups, so that I can compensate for students with special needs without creating multiple tests.

to define when an exam is open (available) and closed in one form, so I do not need to navigate to other pages/forms.

the grade book to ignore assignments not yet due, so that the course grades reflect the students' current standing.

to allow students to grade their own or others work, so that I can see the reflection, assessment criteria and peers standards used by students.

to manually enter/overwrite grades in the grade book, so that the automatic calculations within the grade book or from the assignment are ignored.

to define grading criteria for each assignment and the course, so that the grade book automatically calculates final grades.

to return to my last edited entry in the gradebook so that I can quickly make my edits to my gradebook.

to use an evaluation tool that allows for mixing multiple choice and open-ended questions so that I can evaluate my students.

create learning experiences for my students that model a variety of different pedagogies, for example constructivism, active learning, student centered learning, collaborative learning, etc. so that we meet the needs of different learner styles and types.

As an Instructional Designer, I want...

would like to pass grades from the LMS to the SIS, so that faculty do not need to manually add their course grades.

As a Student, I want...

the option of showing everyone's grades in the class anonymously, so that students can compare their grades with the rest of the class.

to view my individual grades for assignments, so I can understand how my total grade is affected.

to view my course grades throughout the term, so I can see my standing in the course.

view all of my grades across all courses, so I so not need to enter each course.

As a Trainer, I want...

to use secure exam tools so that I can administer exam to both online and in-person students.

access subject-matter specific materials, so that I can become a more proficient trainer.

4 Course Management

As a Faculty Member, I want...

to add individual students who have not enrolled in my course section, so that they can audit the course.

to add access for tutors, so that they can assist students working in the course.

to manipulate items/icons on a course page using a simple drag-drop interface, so that I don't have to click through the LMS interface.

native drag and drop content directly from my desktop into my course sisette, so that I don't have to click the desktop operating system's navigational interface.

create learning experiences for my students that model a variety of different pedagogies, for example constructivism, active learning, student centered learning, collaborative learning, etc.,so that I can meet the needs of different learner styles and types.

varying content presented to different students in my course, so that I can construct individualized curricula for my students depending on assessment measures.

a "confirmation of receipt," so that I know that a student has received and opened an e-mail sent from the LMS.

to organize all of my course materials by weekly session, so that students can determine which assignments have been completed for each week in the proper order.

to toggle my course back and forth from faculty to student view, so I can verify that materials I've developed will function as designed.

to select multiple attributes associated with my course (including user ID, group membership, date range, and grade book results), so that I can control the visibility of course items.

to define release criteria for my content in my course, so that I can assign work to my students based on specific dates, to specific groups and/or specific grading criteria.

to create groups using sign-up sheets, so that students can self-identify for activities within the LMS.

to create groups of students within the course, so that I can manage their activities (access to content, tools).

to remove students from my course individually, so that I can remove students when they have dropped during the initial weeks of the semester.

to uploading files in two clicks, so that I do not need to navigate through various windows.

find a discussion post in two clicks, so that I do not need to navigate through various windows.

reset course materials for the next semester in two clicks, so that I do not need to navigate through various windows.

to publish multiple sections of the same course, so that uniform/standard content can be viewed by different users in different sections.

to administer course sections independently, so that modifications in one section do not affect other sections.

to track student participation in learning activities, so I can assess student engagement and time on task.

to view all input from an individual student from a single screen (e.g. see assignments, discussion posts, assessment attempts etc.), so that I can assess activity and completeness.

to create new courses/sections at any time and independent of the SIS, so I can develop course sites on the fly for my own use.

to save/transfer announcements from semester to semester, so that I can create a repository of effective messages for a class.

authorized users (e.g. faculty, course/department chair) to add access to courses, so that the department can facilitate peer observations.

set access time (start and end dates) for non-enrolled users (guests to the course), so that they can be removed without manual intervention.

students to work within the tools where assignments are delivered, so work their work is saved automatically and associated with the assignment (they do not have to attach their documents/drafts/final).

to download my course, so I can view my course off-line on my desktop computer.

to set access dates (opening and closing) for all discussions, so I do not need to individually open or close a discussion manually when the date arrives.

view compatible 3rd party/external applications/widgets within one location of the LMS, so I can add non-LMS native functionality to my course.

access to my courses from previous semesters, so I can use the old course format/content to start planning and building for the next semester.

to select old/current course content to populate new courses, so I do not have to manually add or create them again.

record the attendance in my in-person course in the LMS, so I can include participation in the online grade book.

to export reports on student activity, so I can share information with non LMS users.

to run reports on page use for various components of my course so that I can measure who's accessing what and for how long.

to globally change dates within my course for new semesters, so that I do not have to change each manually for each event/due-date.

access and change dates within my course through a single calendar view, so that I do not need to navigate to each event to change dates.

view all attributes associated with creating/releasing assignments, discussions, exams, etc., so I do not need to navigate to other pages to develop and distribute content.

to open access to all or some of my course (LMS tools, activities, content), so that the public can participate in my course.

access to permissions/attributes for each tool in the LMS, so that I can control which tools students have access to.

to toggle between courses so that I can control the visibility to all of my courses.

to migrate existing course material to new teaching and learning environment so that I can continue teaching online.

create learning experiences for my students that model a variety of different pedagogies, for example constructivism, active learning, student centered learning, collaborative learning, etc. so that we meet the needs of different learner styles and types.

have a learning platform that is accepted by QualityMatters.org so that distance learning courses can continue to gain approval from this organization.

As an LMS Administrator, I want...

to open access to all or some of the LMS courses (LMS tools, activities, content), so that the public can participate in the courses.

As a Student, I want...

open different sections in different windows of the LMS, so that I am able to view class materials from multiple courses/classes.

a "How do I..." glossary, so that I can look for answers to my problems.

to open multiple browser windows, so that I can see independent courses or parts of the same course in different windows.

to be notified of activity in the LMS via communications channels outside of the LMS, so that I know when changes to the course have been made.

to access the LMS from the SIS and/or my campus email account, so I do not have to log in again.

see the status of my assignments, so I can see work that is in progress or completed.

access to last year's course material so that I can prepare for my qualifying examination.

to have a calendar-based course site so that I can view all of my course material depending on the date.

to search across all of my courses so that I can easily access my course materials and information.

to have the same look and feel within a program or college so that my course will be consistent.

to search all courses simultaneously so that I can document that key concepts and objectives are being covered (in an environment where all courses are team taught).

to post an online searchable handbook so that users can download and easily print forms.

have a learning platform that allows me to get critical, up-to-the-minute SIS information about my student status such as registration data, grade reports, billing info. etc so that I don't have to log in separately.

have a more sophisticated, faster, and technologically advanced system that uses podcasts, lectures, and streams entertaining presentations that use animation so that I can get a better learning environment along with a better experience.

5 Content Management & Multi-Media

As a Faculty Member, I want...

to include audio and video files to my course, so that students can access each independently without leaving the LMS to use another application.

both students and me to create and save oral presentations (audio) from within the LMS, so that we do not need to log into other applications or upload 3rd party files.

access to a synchronous communications tool (e.g. real time audio, video, whiteboard, presentation, application sharing, break out rooms, and archiving capabilities) within the LMS, so I do not need to re-authenticate when moving between systems.

to upload and distribute media from different sources within the course, so that the location of the content is transparent to the instructor and students.

a student specific content repositories per course, so that submitted files can be segregated from other student work and retained in the course.

to sort student files in a course by author, date, title, etc., so that students and faculty can find files based on various known information.

to view the versions of submitted or collaborative work, so I can assess which edits where made by various contributors and when.

to access multiple drafts of content created in the LMS, so that my students and I can review previous work.

upload multiple files and file types per assignment, so I can present independent, but related documents and students can submit independent but related files.

to post homework assignments and solutions, so that my students have access to them.

to delete an incomplete post or mishandled assignment, so that so that it is not included in grading.

content created within the LMS during a course by students to be exportable, so that students can transport artifacts to other personal or institutional systems.

to open, comment on and save student documents, all with in the LMS, so that students can view my edits without downloading and uploading files.

to see the duration time of audio files accessible in the course, so I can sort recordings from longest to shortest.

edit content (tests or assessments) within the LMS after students have submitted work, so I can correct errors and republish rather than create new tests/assignments.

to export my course materials, so that any other instructor in my institution can use them.

drag and drop assignment/content, so that I do not need to click a series of buttons/links/pages to order my documents/activities.

to group media content uploaded to the LMS, so that I can see objects in relationship to each section, course, user.

a standards based interface, so I can import course content from publishers, test generators, or other sources.

to allow peers access to selected work, so that students can review one another's work.

access and store content independently of the course/section, directly from within the LMS, so I do not need to log into or navigate to another system.

embed (not just link) Web 0 technologies, so I can customize my course with existing technologies.

to model face to face interactions online so that I can have small group work sessions and large group facilitated discussions.

As an Instructional Designer, I want...

to upload a file, multiple files or all files in a folder at once, so I do not have to upload files individually.

As a Librarian, I want...

to embed library e-reserves directly in courses, so students and faculty do not need to log into another system to access content.

a repository to upload cross-course resources, so faculty, nor I, need to load it into each course/section.

As a Student, I want...

to provide access to my content, tools and activities to other students, so I can collaborate with student teams within the course.

to access synchronous communication tools within a course and outside of a course, so that I can work with classmates on my own.

embed (not just link) Web 0 technologies, so I can customize my course with existing technologies.

to accomplish course administrative tasks (like uploading files, finding a discussion post, resetting course material for the next semester, etc.) in two clicks from within the specific feature, so that I can maintain a contextual work flow.

to create a portfolio, so that I can selectively extract content from any of my courses and allow external visitors to view it.

the LMS to save my work automatically and periodically, so that I can access my previous work without it being lost due to a timeout or outage.

a "light" version of the system, so that my dial-up connection will not get bogged down.

a mobile version of the system, so that I can access my courses on my hand held device

standards compliant audio/video formats available through multiple players, so that I can use my own audio/video player (desktop, hand held) to listen to class audio/video files.

video or lecture capture within the LMS, so that I do not need to access (perhaps logging into) multiple systems.

the files I post to reflect the time zone that I am in, so that I do not lose out on the amount of time to complete assignments.

the files posted my others (including faculty) to reflect the time zone that I am in, so that I do not lose out on the amount of time to view materials.

to move the tools within the interface, so that I can to avoid "scrolling" the window.

to view all of my course lectures, so that I can determine their order within the course.

a single reference for all of my courses, so I can see (and access) current due dates for assignments and tests/quizzes, and updates when due dates change.

new notifications for new content and grades to disappear after I have looked at them, so I know what is still awaiting review.

to aggregate dates associated with LMS content and activity with my other calendars, so I can view personal and academic events despite which calendar I am in.

archive my courses, so that I can access content from within.

create and maintain local archives and backups, so that I can store and access course content despite my campuses or systems policies.

to share my uploaded documents and LMS-specific content through the LMS, so my classmates can work with me in our own study groups.

personal areas to develop and store content, so others cannot access my class notes, drafts, uploaded files, etc.

to submit multiple drafts of assignments through the LMS, so instructors can provide feedback before the final grade for the assignment.

to access campus related links in (# of clicks) so that I can easily locate relevant articles.

to take an online course from another campus so that I don't have to apply to their program and get a second ID.

6 Accessibility & Usability

As a Faculty Member, I want...

user-adjustable font sizes and audio tools, so that students with special needs can access my course and content.

to tailor the interface and functionality, so that I can employ principles of universal design in the development of my course.

access the LMS in any browser, so that I can work on my course from any networked computer.

to customize the icons for tools in my course, so I and students can set up the user interface to our personal preferences.

to customize the icons for tools in my language courses, so that students can work in the language of study.

cross-platform compatibility, so that I can use the LMS on multiple devices and computers (PC/Mac/Linux, hand helds, smartphones, tablets).

508 and WAI compliant and certification, so that I can conform with local, state and federal accessibility policies and regulations.

FERPA complaint security, so that I can conform with local, state and federal policies and regulations.

As a Student, I want

to contact someone over the phone for troubleshooting, so that I can talk to a human being and get the problem fixed faster and easier.

access help, tips/tricks from within each tool/feature, so that I can get help in context to the LMS functionality.

to allow students to change their username within the course to a nickname, so that students don't have to show their full name.

to access, review and edit the course through audio only, so that visually impaired students can participate in online courses.

non-visual cues/interfaces for all activities undertaken in the LMS and the content delivered through it, so that I can access all functionality and materials within the course.

7 System Administration

As an LMS Administrator, I want...

to add individual students who have not enrolled in my course section, so that they can audit the course.

to restrict course design to a lead teacher, so that other instructors of a section teaching that course cannot alter specific elements.

to provide templates for courses, so that the look and feel within a program or college can be consistent.

to view all links to an individual resource from the source item, so I can click a file to see where in the course it is being used.

the option to delete the source file/activity when the link to the file/activity is deleted, so I do not have orphaned files in the system.

to move or rename files, so that links do not break.

to upload a file, multiple files or all files in a folder at once, so I do not have to upload files individually.

upload files via common standards from within the LMS, so that I do not have to use multiple applications.

a unique identifier associated with files, so I can identify the person who uploaded a file.

file creation/modified dates to remain intact after a course is copied for reuse in subsequent semesters, so I can find the history of files.

warnings for html files that have encodings that do not match_, so that errors can be addressed before course pages are published publicly._

to parse file names when uploading, so that improper formatting can be detected.

to export content or learning activities in the course in standard formats (e.g. SCORM, Common Cartridge, pdf, .docx, .rtf) with the option to include student content, so that learning objects and archived materials may be used in the future.

to export documents from the course in standard formats (e.g. SCORM, Common Cartridge, pdf, .docx, .rtf) with the option to include student content, so that learning objects and archived materials may be used independantly on the desktop in a office productivity tools.

to create/edit html documents through the LMS or a third-party html editor without leaving the LMS, so that I do not have to manage multiple applications, file copies or logins.

to set the page I return to after undertaking an activity (clicking "Submit" or "Save" in a form), so that I do not have to navigate from the system's default refresh page.

to bookmark specific pages, so I can return to pages where I undertake common tasks.

cross list the same course, so that one course or one section can be offered by different academic departments.

batch upload my students and my courses either on a " as requested basis" or all at once, so I do not need to manually and individually make modifications to the course/section/LMS.

to pass userid's and passwords from other campus enterprise applications to the LMS, so users do not need to remember multiple logins.

to retain student data when students are un-enrolled from courses, so that I can review their activity and content when they are no longer able to access the course/section/LMS.

to back and restore courses and content (individually and in bulk), so that I can provide faculty with up-to-date versions of their courses and content in case they lose or delete information.

to query courses, so that I can find specific students names, groups, file names/types, text strings, dates, etc.

an open database, so that I can construct my own data queries and reports or modify the systems default queries/reports.

define the features (tools, functionality) at the institutional level, so I do not need to go into each course to add or remove tools/features/functionality individually.

setup default grading schema at the institution level, so I do not need to set up grading in each course/section individually.

to implement custom branding at the institutional and departmental levels, so I do not need to edit each course/section individually.

to pass enrollment information automatically from the SIS, so that courses, students, etc. are updated in real-time and I do not need to manage batch uploads.

to integrate the LMS with identity management standards (e.g. CAS, Shibboleth, etc.), so that I can manage authentication and authorization consistently across all of my campus services.

to provide users with immediate course registration so that users can quickly access their content.

access, assess, and manage permissions for ePortfolio content directly from within the LMS, so I do not need to log into or navigate to another system.

to have a system that allows incomplete access for individual students once a course has closed.

to use discussion topics from another section so that I do not have to manually copy and paste from one course to the next.

to need to track authorship of course content as course sections are copied and edited over the life of a course.

As an Instructional Designer, I want...

to automate the creation of a blank course shells for every course, so that faculty are not required to fill out a form.

to automate the creation of a blank course shells for every course, so that administrators do not have to create batches for course shell creation by hand.

to enter_/view_ courses without enrolling in the course roster, so I do not appear in areas like the grade book, student roster, etc.

to manage enrollments and privileges to courses from a central location, so I do not have to log in to or access each course separately.

to integrate with external and internal resources with a single sign on (e.g. content management, wikis, blogs, eportfolio, directory services, student information systems, etc.), so that users do not have to log in multiple times to multiple systems.

to pass information from and to the SIS through common and diverse methods simultaneously within the same instance, so that campuses can use integration methods within their capacity and resources.

a system with contextually-sensitive help combined with built-in screencast tutorials for better self-help remediation.

8 Migration

As an Instructional Designer, I want...

to import courses archived from other LMS's, so that we can respond quickly and efficiently to faculty requests for new course shells from legacy systems or systems on other campuses.

to batch import archived courses from other LMS's, so that we can respond quickly and efficiently to faculty requests for new course shells from legacy systems or systems on other campuses.

to script translation criteria and batch load courses for migration, so that I do not need to manually address each course to be converted.

an standardized implementation plan that has been tested and verifiable from other similar institutions, so that the campuses can be up and running with an LMS solution within 18 months

3 Administrative and Technical Requirements

3.1 Application Administration

As an LMS administrator, I want...

access to individual user accounts (profiles/attributes) within the LMS, so that I can make manually view and update users, information, roles, sections, courses, enrollments.

to create individual user accounts (profiles/attributes) within the LMS, so that I add users, information, roles, sections and courses outside of the batch process.

system-wide access to UID, groups, courses, sections, so that I can manually resolve issues.

access to LMS vendor-sponsored/supported technical training, so that I can stay abreast of the technical developments required to support the LMS.

to participate in peer-to-peer communities of practice, so that I can learn from and communicate with other LMS users.

to send announcements to users of the system so they can be informed of system outages, issues or scheduled maintenance events.

3.2 Identity Management: Authentication & Authorization

As an LMS administrator, I want...

the LMS to authenticate against external LDAP sources, so that hosted campuses can manage their own users and credentials.

to set user authentication independently of, and in addition to, external LDAP sources, so that I can set local access.

to pass authentication and authorization from the LMS, so that courses can include third-party tools.

3.3 Course, Section, User Batching

As an LMS administrator, I want...

a secure FTP directory that multiple unique campuses can upload batch files to, so that the LMS can access and create courses.

a secure FTP directory that multiple unique campuses can upload batch files to, so that the LMS can access and create users.

a secure FTP directory that multiple unique campuses can upload batch files to, so that the LMS can access and create roles (instructional designers, instructors, students, LMS administrators, teaching assistants, auditors, help desk staff).

batched users to be enrolled in their courses by the LMS, so we and the campuses do not have to do it manually.

3.4 Backup

As an LMS administrator, I want...

to back up individual active sections on a weekly bases, so that UMassOnline can restore individual courses and course content on demand.

to archive individual sections on a semester bases from the LMS, so that UMassOnline can distribute courses/sections/content to the campuses for archiving.

a back-up of the entire database, so that UMassOnline can restore our implementation for disaster recovery.

3.5 Continuity

As a technical operations manager, I want...

to be notified when LMS service interruptions occur, so that I can notify our stakeholders.

to be notified when LMS service is depreciated, so that I can notify our stakeholders.

users to fail over upon a service outage to a redundant environment, so that I can ensure continued availability of the LMS.

to sync my production and disaster recovery environments, so that I can ensure data continuity at the time of a disaster.

to stand up a new primary production environment in the event of a disaster within one day, so that we will have minimal down time.

a pre-defined maintenance and upgrade schedule, so I can coordinate with multiple campuses maintenance windows and upgrades in a consistent manner.

real time notifications, so I can communicate with users immediately of system issues while they are logged in to the LMS.

to emulate the user experience (all roles), so that I can monitor the health of the LMS periodically.

to monitor LMS resource consumption (CPU, bandwidth I/O, data base I/O, etc.), so that I can ascertain health of the system and its resources.

to review LMS resource consumption (CPU, bandwidth I/O, data base I/O, etc.), so I can diagnose service degradation and interruptions.

to monitor user activity (active users, http requests, sessions open, etc.), so I can assess systems performance based on demand.

to access feature by feature comparisons related to functional upgrades so that I can train and support end-users in a context that is familiar to them.

3.6 Systems Integration

As an LMS administrator, I want...

to expose available third-party tools through the internal LMS tool set, so that faculty can find available tools within the LMS itself.

to pass course/section attributes (user identity, section enrollment, course information, etc.) from the LMS, so that courses can include third-party tools.

to include contact information (email, chat and phone) within each page of a course section, so that users can connect directly through the LMS to support services.

to integrate with campus student information systems frequently, so UMassOnline that can ensure the timely transfer of data.

to create courses, sections and users (all roles) in real time, so campuses can provide on-demand enrollments.

to provide access to third-party tools (Helix, Wimba, SafeAssign, Scholar, Respondus, Voice Tools) from within the LMS, so that users can move seamlessly between UMassOnline's current portfolio of systems.

to transfer files between the LMS and third-party tools (Helix, Wimba, SafeAssign, Scholar, Respondus, Voice Tools), so that content can move seamlessly between UMassOnline's current portfolio of systems.

to integrate the internal email of the LMS and the email address of record in the student information system (or another preferred email address), so users can manage a single email account.

access within the LMS to all data fields published by the student information system, so I can create standard or customized levels and points of integration.

3.7 User Activity and Performance Reporting

As an LMS administrator, I want...

to query the number of logged in users via the LMS, so that we can assess current and historical load measurements.

to query the frequency LMS specific tools are used, via the LMS, so that we can understand user activity and potentially needs (training, technical, 3rd party tools, etc.) for enhancements.

to assess LMS activity (time on task/page), student activity (enter/exit page), enrollments, sections, and tool/item use via the LMS, so that we can generate general utilization reports and specifically determine if access has been attained by users.

to search sections and users based on the LMS's attributes/criteria, via the LMS, so that we can build ad hoc reports.

to design and modify existing default reports, via the LMS, so that we can build ad hoc reports.

to query LMS generated schema/data via an open database, so that I can run reports via a third party reporting tool.

3.8 Testing & QA

As an LMS QA technician, I want...

to access a test environment that emulates our production environment, so I can assess reported issues/bugs, updates, patches, enhancements, etc. without affecting the production environment and our active users.

to view the LMS as multiple user-types in the same login session without logging in and out, so that I can emulate our user's experiences and test functionality across the system.

to participate in beta and cohort programs so I can evaluate patches and fixes alongside a community of peers.

3.9 Training

As a system-wide trainer, I want...

to provide campuses with training materials that focus on side-by-side feature comparisons with Blackboard Vista, so that UMassOnline and our supported campuses can train campuses in the new LMS environment.

to modify vendor created training materials, so I can address UMassOnline's unique service environment that campuses have up-to-date, authoritative reference materials per patch, dotX version, service packs, etc.

to modify vendor created training materials, so I can address UMassOnline's unique service/support environment.

access to LMS vendor-sponsored/supported training related to pedagogical (teaching and learning) affordances, so that I can educate local campus trainers and faculty on how to support unique teaching styles.

access to LMS vendor-sponsored/supported functional training, so that UMassOnline can educate local campus trainers and end-users with point and click functionality.

to participate in peer-to-peer communities of practice, so that I can learn from, and communicate with, other campuses using the same LMS.

access to LMS vendor-sponsored/supported technical training, so I can stay up to date on administrative, integration and technical issues.

in-line contextual help, so that users can resolve their own usability/feature/functionality issues.

prompts/hints when users mouse-over objects, so that users can learn about previously, or infrequently, used tools/features.

to provide users access to tips and tricks, so that users can become more proficient with the LMS.

access for all users to a community of practice, so they can learn from peers.

user to have access to subject-matter specific tutorials, so that users can become more proficient.

3.10 Technical and End User Support

As an LMS administrator, I want...

to contribute our local technical and user support discoveries to the support provider, so that their knowledge base reflects current issues/understanding/resolutions of the user community.

to download release notes from a secure web site to create testable scripts, so I can assess production readiness for hotfixes, patches, service packs and upgrades.

As a support analyst, I want...

access to a ticketing system, so that I can report to, update, search for, etc. issues directly with the service provider.

issue status (eg: bug tracking/resolution) communications through the ticketing system, so that I can document and communicate to my end-users.

to include multiple user types from our community in service requests/tickets, so that affected users are communicated regarding status updates and during issue resolution.

to participate in peer-to-peer communities of practice, so that I can learn from and communicate with other LMS users.

to access the system under different roles in the same login session, so I do not have to log out and back in several times to assess issues.

to reach a support technician immediately, so I can report system outages 24/

to reach a support technician within 30 minutes, so I can report performance degradation that falls below the SLA.

to reach a support technician within 30 minutes, so I can report when major components (content/activity) are unavailable/unusable.

to reach a support technician within 1 hour, so I can report when minor components (formatting/functionality) are operating abnormally.

to reach a support technician within 30 minutes, so I can report performance degradation that falls below the SLA.

to propose product enhancements/feature requests, so I can help direct and shape product development to meet our users' needs.

4 Program Management

4.1 Communications

As a Academic Program Manager, I want...

to send messages/announcements through the LMS based on course/student attributes (course, program, status, major, etc), so we can target specific student populations.

to determine who is online and accessing course content/activities, so I can verify submitted work.

4.2 Budgeting

As an Academic Program Manager, I want...

access to contracted pricing and services, so that pricing is stable and service is constant over time.

4.3 Quality

As an Academic Program Manager, I want...

to provide access to departmental staff, so I can conduct peer reviews of courses.

4.4 Service & Support

As an Academic Program Manager, I want...

performance and response definitions with criteria and metrics, so that service and support can be monitored, measured and reported to any interested stakeholders.

performance and response definitions with remedies for degraded service, so that the campus has recourse for poor service/support.

to verify ADA compliance, so I can meet University, State and Federal regulations.

4.5 Training

As an Instructional Designer, I want...

to cover fundamental training on the new LMS features and functionality_ for faculty in two hours, so that they can deliver a recently migrated course as is.

training resources, including syllabi/ outlines, powerpoints, tutorials, and QuickStart guides, so I do not have to develop them on my own.

Made in the USA
Middletown, DE
13 June 2021

42148114R00064